Praise for MORE Equine Law
by Julie I. Fershtman, Atto

"Once again Julie Fershtman provides e
guide to safety and success as she helps us m
we can avoid. She is an extraordinary writer. . , practical,
and to-the-point. This book is a must for *anyone* involved with horses."

Barbra Schulte
International Clinician and
Author of Cutting, One Run at a Time

"Horse owners and professionals can play ostrich and hope nothing
ever goes wrong, or they can study *MORE Equine Law & Horse Sense* and be
forewarned and prepared. A great service to the horse industry."

Denny Emerson
Master Instructor, Olympic Rider,
Member, Executive Committee of the
American Horse Shows Association

"Explanations of the law that make sense to every day life. Julie I.
Fershtman does it again! This is a practical book every horse owner should
read and own."

Kandee Haertel, Executive Director
Equestrian Land Conservation Resource

"In today's world, every participant in sport should receive guidance
regarding legal ramifications of participation. *MORE Equine Law & Horse
Sense* should be required reading for all instructors."

Michael O. Page
Master Instructor, Olympic Medalist,
Former Chef d'Equipe of the U.S. Equestrian Team

"Another learning tool for EVERYONE and ANYONE in the horse industry! Easy to read and understand. I recommend this book for quality
horse business guidelines."

Lynn Palm
International Instructor, Horse Trainer, Author, and Competitor

"This book is a comprehensive and valuable resource for people in the
horse industry. It is written in a user-friendly format. It gives examples of
problems that people experience in the real world and how to avoid them."

Larry Anton
President, Horse Industry Alliance

"*MORE Equine Law & Horse Sense* provides legal information that brings
the horse industry into the year 2000. Every horseman, horsewoman, and
their legal advisers should purchase this book and refer to it often to aid in
decision-making that may help them avoid expensive and troublesome liability problems in the future."

Linda Liestman, President
North American Horsemen's Association

"*MORE Equine Law & Horse Sense* is a book all horsemen should have and read. It is very easy to see why Julie Fershtman is 'The Best of the Best' in her field."

Richard Shrake
Judge, Clinician, and Author of Resistance Free Riding *and* Western Horsemanship

"Julie Fershtman's newest book, *MORE Equine Law & Horse Sense*, is another invaluable source of user-friendly, well-organized, easy-to-read, essential legal information for all of us in the horse industry. Whether you are a long-time professional or a first-time horse-owner, you need to own this book. And if you don't yet own her first book, *Equine Law & Horse Sense*, you should buy that one too. They're informational, enjoyable, and can help save you money and keep you out of trouble. What could be better than that?"

Jessica Jahiel, Ph.D.
National Clinician/ Author of Several Books,
Including Riding for the Rest of Us

"*MORE Equine Law & Horse Sense* should be a required read for anyone in the horse industry today! Breeders, trainers, riding instructors, business owners and operators will receive a wealth of timely and valuable information. Page for page, *MORE Equine Law & Horse Sense* is definitely 'Best of Show'! You will reference it again and again."

LaJuan Skiver, Executive Director
Certified Horsemanship Association (CHA)

"Today's horse hobbyist or professional must know certain facts to prevent trouble with the marshal and with neighbors. Julie Fershtman's new book, *MORE Equine Law and Horse Sense*, effectively corrals pertinent legal issues for us and puts them in terms we all can understand. She "demythtifies" insurance, gives contract advice, discusses zoning, tells us how to avoid liability and much more. We are lucky to have Julie Fershtman. Buy her book."

Cherry Hill
Author of 23 Books on Horse Training and Care

"Julie Fershtman has done it again! Her new book – a follow-up to her unique *Equine Law & Horse Sense* – is full of essential legal information for today's horse people, amateur or professional. Clear, practical guidelines for understanding and avoiding common equine legal problems, in user-friendly language. This book can save you time, money, and costly mistakes!"

Susan Harris
National Clinician/Author of The U.S. Pony Clubs Manual *and* Grooming to Win

"Thanks to attorney Julie Fershtman, horse owners and members of the equine business community no longer have to wonder what their legal rights are and how to protect them. *MORE Equine Law & Horse Sense* provides all the legal information a horse person could possibly need, from sales contracts and how to use them, to land use and zoning. With this book, Fershtman has once and for all proven herself to be the legal guardian angel of horse people everywhere."

Audrey Pavia
*Author of "*Horses for Dummies ®*"*

"Once again, Julie Fershtman has filled a great need in the horse industry. Clear, concise information in an easy-to-find format will help instructors, stable owners, and all those who own just a horse or two, to answer legal and business questions as they arise. This is a *valuable* book."

Charlotte Brailey Kneeland
Director, American Riding Instructors Association

"*MORE Equine Law & Horse Sense* is a step by step 'pound of prevention.' By providing easy to understand explanations of legal considerations, this informative guide diffuses the intimidation factor that often accompanies the nitty gritty business of horses. [The book] empowers readers to engage in win-win business negotiations."

Peggy Cummings
International Instructor, Author of Connected Riding

"*MORE Equine Law & Horse Sense* is an outstanding reference and companion to *Equine Law & Horse Sense*. ... Julie Fershtman is an extremely credible author in the area of equine law, and has brought these issues to producers and horse owners in a very timely fashion. I require these texts for students and highly recommend them to all horse owners and owners of equine related businesses."

Lance A. Baker, Ph.D.
Assistant Professor - Equine Industry Program,
West Texas A & M University
AQHA Judge

"I consider Julie Fershtman to be the leading authority on Equine Law. Her ability to put legal language into everyday terms provides all of us in the equine industry with the knowledge to avoid unnecessary problems and expenses. The cost of her books will be returned to me many times over."

Rick Sykes
Co-Founder and Chief Operating Officer,
National Barrel Horse Association

"This book has something useful for every horse facility owner, and expands on Julie Fershtman's first indispensable book. Another winner!"

Dru Malavase
Chair, New York State Horse Council Safety Committee
Chair, ASTM Committee on Equestrian Protective Headgear

"*MORE Equine Law & Horse Sense* presents a wealth of material in a clear and logical manner. As a horseman, teacher, and expert witness, the information that Julie Fershtman has provided is both important and essential. The book . . . is presented in a way that makes it interesting."

Kathy Kusner
Olympic Rider, National and International Instructor,
Expert Witness

"Julie Fershtman's new book, *MORE Equine Law & Horse Sense*, should be added to that small shelf containing her first book and just a few other essential reference books that every smart horseman in this business has right behind their desk. *MORE Equine Law & Horse Sense* is ... more of the "what if's" and "how comes" that we're likely to encounter if we stay in this business long enough. Written with real-life scenarios, *MORE Equine Law & Horse Sense* is easy reading with concise passages giving valuable advice to avoid lots of grief. Take my advice and get both of Ms. Fershtman's books."

Steven J. Bennett
Executive Director, Horsemanship Safety Association

"An essential reference for every horse person's bookshelf. Includes useful details for the recreational and professional horse person, as well as associations. Provides excellent direction for developing legal documents .... Interesting examples make it extremely readable. Julie Fershtman has done it again!"

Roberta "Bobbi" Lipka
AHSA Judge & 1993 Recipient of
American Horse Council's Van Ness Award

"This book is a must have for the shelf of any professional or amateur horse trainer. It's horse law for the layman in understandable terms."

Jan Dawson, J.D.
President, American Association for Horsemanship Safety

"*MORE Equine Law & Horse Sense* extends the information presented by Julie Fershtman, attorney equine law, in her previous excellent book *Equine Law & Horse Sense*."

Doris Bixby Hammett, M.D.
Board Member, American Medical Equestrian Association

"It is your horse, ultimately, who will benefit from Julie Fershtman's new legal handbook for horseowners. She did an excellent job on a subject that is notoriously difficult for the lay person to understand. Now, thanks to Julie's thoughtful presentation of laws that govern our routine actions, we can actually appreciate it."

Leslie Desmond
Horsemanship Coach and Author

·MORE·
Equine & Law
HORSE SENSE

Julie I. Fershtman
ATTORNEY AT LAW

HORSES & THE LAW PUBLISHING
P.O. Box 250696
Franklin, Michigan 48025-0696

*To my daughter Katie
and the ribbons and trophies that come naturally
when we live life to its fullest.*

Warning and Disclaimer

PLEASE READ CAREFULLY

This book is sold with the understanding that neither the author, publisher, nor distributor are engaged in rendering legal services. Legal advice is given during a mutually-established attorney-client relationship where a client gives an attorney specific facts. If legal or other expert assistance is required, the services of a competent professional should be sought.

This book is also not intended to encourage you to become a "do-it-yourself" lawyer. However, it may help you to work better with an attorney to achieve your goals.

Please keep in mind that the general legal principles discussed in this book may differ in each state, and exceptions may exist. The continuing challenge of the practice of law is that laws constantly change and new cases continue to be decided.

The author and Horses & The Law Publishing shall have neither liability nor responsibility to any person or entity with respect to any loss or damage caused, or alleged to be caused, directly or indirectly, by the information contained in this book.

If you do not wish to be bound by the above, you may return this book to the publisher for a full refund.

Contents

Chapter Four
Relationships with Others Involving Horses—Boarding, Training, Sharing, and Leasing Horses

Chapter Five
Selecting and Managing an Equine Business

Chapter Six
Land Use and Zoning Issues

Chapter Seven
Equine Liabilities—The Latest Developments and How to Avoid Liability

About the Author

Julie I. Fershtman is one of the best-known lawyers in the country serving many facets of the horse industry. Her law practice, based in Bingham Farms, Michigan, crosses all equine breeds and disciplines and serves stables, professionals, businesses, show managers, insurers, associations, and individual horse owners across the United States. She also serves as a national legal consultant.

An attorney since 1986, Ms. Fershtman has received many professional honors. In 1995 the American Bar Association's *Barrister Magazine* named her one of "21 Young Lawyers Leading the Nation Into The 21st Century." In 1997, the Certified Horsemanship Association (CHA) awarded her its National Partner in Safety Award. In 1998, the American Riding Instructors Association presented her with an "Outstanding Achievement" Award.

Ms. Fershtman has lectured in over 20 states at conventions that include Equitana, American Horse Council, National Equine Law Conference, Equine Affaire, EQWest, and the American Riding Instructors' Association Convention. She is the legal consultant to *EQUUS Magazine* and an "Ask the Expert" consultant for *Horse & Rider* and *Practical Horseman* magazines. Her articles have appeared in over 70 different publications and web sites.

Over the years, she has achieved several noteworthy courtroom successes on legal matters affecting the horse industry and has drafted hundreds of contracts. The *Martindale-Hubbell Law Directory* awarded her an "AV" rating, its highest rating. She is also listed in *Who's Who in American Law*.

A horse enthusiast for over 30 years, she has earned awards and championships in horse shows. She resides with her husband and daughter in Franklin, Michigan, where they have a small, suburban horse facility.

Preface

Another book on equine law? Let's face it, legal topics can be hard to understand. And if we understand them, they can seem boring. Even worse, legal topics can be unpleasant because they tend to involve bitter disputes, shattered relationships, and the sometimes tragic misfortunes of others.

Should we care about legal issues? As a horse enthusiast for more than 30 years, and a lawyer for 14 of them, I strongly believe that we should care about them. The fact is, whether we like it or not, the law impacts almost everything we do with horses. For example, when we buy the stable of our dreams or the land to build it, we face land use laws (explained in Chapter 6). Or, we wonder what the law says if a boarding stable gives our horse substandard care (see Chapter 4). We all worry about getting sued if our horse hurts someone, especially since people say that states have "zero liability laws." (Chapters 7 and 8 cover this, and Chapter 10 discusses insurance.) Equine professionals know that laws affect them but they are often too busy to learn them. (Chapter 5 of this book gives a good start.) As men and women who enjoy horses, we need more information that explains legal issues in a way that we can understand. This is why, four years after I released my last book, *Equine Law & Horse Sense*, I now offer you more.

Welcome to *MORE Equine Law & Horse Sense*. This book gives you more—more lessons in the law, more ways to avoid conflict, and more ways to know when, and how, to seek out professional help.

Best wishes for more fun, safety, and success in your horse activities.

Julie I. Fershtman
Bingham Farms, Michigan
January 2000

INTRODUCTION

WHAT IS EQUINE LAW?

Equine law cannot easily be defined. In its most basic sense, it is law that involves virtually all aspects of horses and horse-related activities. It also involves people who enjoy horses or make a living from them, such as horse owners, businesses, professionals, associations and facilities.

Like doctors who specialize in a particular type of medicine, equine law attorneys are lawyers who have gone beyond general practice to develop special expertise in horse activities and the laws concerning them. Lawyers who practice equine law can help with several things including:

- Draft, review, or negotiate equine-related contracts (such as purchase and sale agreements, leases, stallion service contracts, liability waivers/releases, and boarding contracts)
- Set up corporations, partnerships, syndications, or Limited Liability Companies
- Assist with tax planning, and resolving tax disputes with the government
- Help plan and document real estate purchases or transactions
- Represent people who are threatened with expulsion or suspension from racetracks or associations due to alleged rule violations, or positive drug tests (or represent the associations)
- Handle or resolve zoning and land use disputes
- Help avoid liability through risk-management programs
- Represent people or businesses when disputes or lawsuits arise out of any of the matters described above

This book will help you understand many facets of equine law. It will make you better equipped to assess your needs, plan ahead, take precautions to avoid conflicts, and know when to seek out professional guidance. Much of the information you will learn can help you cut your costs when, and if, you eventually need professional help.

As you will learn, you can handle many simple legal matters on your own. But the complexities of the law may find you—sooner or later—seeking out a lawyer, even if only on a limited basis. Read on to learn how to find the right lawyer when, and if, the need arises.

CHAPTER ONE

MAKING EQUINE LAW ACCESSIBLE AND AFFORDABLE

HOW TO FIND AND HIRE
THE [EQUINE] LAWYER RIGHT FOR YOU

Sooner or later, you may find it to your advantage to hire a lawyer, whether it involves an equine matter or not. When that happens, these are the things you most need to know:

- How to find a lawyer
- How to evaluate which lawyer is right for you
- What to ask the lawyer before hiring him or her
- What do lawyers cost
- What fee arrangements are available
- How to put the attorney-client arrangement in writing
- If a lawyer who practices equine law is better for you than one who does not

Where Can You Find a Lawyer?

Our society is full of lawyers who are seeking your business, each one claiming to be capable of helping you with your legal matter. But how can you find them? Here are some ideas:

Recommendations from other people. Ask your friends, relatives and neighbors if they know of lawyers who practice the type of law for which you seek help.

Recommendations from associations or trade groups. Equine lawyers are often involved in and known by state horse councils, state and local equine associations, breed organizations, and cooperative extension services. Also, equine studies programs might have the names of lawyers who teach courses in equine-related law.

Legal directories. Look for the *Martindale-Hubbell Law Directory* in your local library. Or, visit its web site at: www.martindalehubbell.com, or www.lawyers.com. This directory provides information about lawyers, including: when and where the lawyer went to law school, how long the lawyer has been in practice, areas of expertise and professional accomplishments. Keep in mind that lawyers pay for detailed listings; therefore, you will not find an in-depth listing for every lawyer.

Another benefit of the *Martindale-Hubbell Law Directory* is that it evaluates lawyers. The directory surveys other lawyers and judges in the lawyers' communities to receive ratings of the lawyers' abilities and ethics. The highest available rating is "AV."

Lawyer referral services. Most bar associations (lawyers' organizations) on a state, county, or city level offer lawyer referral services. If you contact the services to request a lawyer practicing in a certain area of the law, they will try to find one or more lawyers on their list to match your request. If you seek a lawyer from these services, the problem is that they usually do not know what "equine law" is and rarely have lawyers listed in these areas. Also, these services refer people only to lawyers pre-registered with their services, leaving out names of numerous other qualified lawyers.

Advertisements. Some lawyers advertise their services in the Yellow Pages, magazines, newsletters and web sites.

How to Evaluate Which Lawyer is Right For You

After you get a name of a qualified lawyer, your search might be over. However, to be sure that you have found someone who can help in your particular situation, take these additional steps:

Make the first call. It may only take a few minutes on the telephone to help you learn that your matter is beyond the lawyer's expertise, that the lawyer might be too expensive, or that you might simply be uncomfortable with him or her. When you call the lawyer, ask questions (several are listed below). Make sure you are satisfied with the answers.

Evaluate the lawyer's style. Do you want your lawyer to bring a certain background, style, or approach to your matter? Depending on the circumstances, for example, you might want a lawyer who is aggressive or who is a recognized expert. Maybe you want someone who shares your interest in resolving your dispute, and who will try to settle it. Or perhaps an experienced lawyer who is well-recognized by the judges in the community is better for your local problem. On the other hand, a lawyer who recently graduated from law school who is willing to take your case at a very low fee in order to develop experience may be just right. You must decide who is best.

Plan a meeting. The first consultation can be done by phone or in person. Consider scheduling a meeting at the lawyer's office, or at a mutually-convenient location. Sometimes seeing the lawyer's office will tell you more about him or her. The office might reveal the lawyer's success, how organized he or she is, and the type of staff and resources available to assist in your legal matter.

Some lawyers charge nothing for the first consultation, but make sure to ask before you show up.

Questions to Ask the Lawyer

To be sure that you have found the right lawyer, ask him or her several questions. Here are some:

- What is your experience in this area of the law? How many cases or matters like mine have you handled?
- Who will be handling my matter – you or someone else at your firm?
- How strong is my case (or defense)? Do you think I have a good chance of winning? Why or why not?
- How often will you let me know about the status of my case?
- Do you have the time to handle my matter?
- Do you have evening or weekend office hours?
- What are the chances that we can resolve this matter out of court, and what might be a reasonable settlement?
- Is my case appropriate for an alternative to the legal system, such as arbitration or mediation? Why or why not?
- How often will you send me bills, and how long will I have to pay them?

Fee Arrangements

Lawyers operate under a variety of fee arrangements. Before you hire a lawyer, make sure that you understand and accept the fee arrangement. Here are the most common ones:

Hourly fee. In most legal matters, you are charged an hourly fee— the lawyer will bill you for each hour of time that he or she spends on your matter. A lawyer's hourly rate will vary according to the lawyer's location, years of experience, reputation, expertise, and many other factors.

When evaluating a lawyer's fee, ask not only the amount he or she charges for each hour of work but also the increments of an hour for which you will be billed. A lawyer who bills you on increments of one-quarter of an hour will cost much more than the lawyer who bills at one-tenth of an hour. For example, if your lawyer charges $150 an hour and you are billed for a five-minute phone call, you will pay $37.50 to the lawyer who bills on quarter-hour increments, but you would only pay $15 to the lawyer who bills on the tenth of an hour.

Contingency fee. Everyone has seen lawyer advertisements promising: "You pay no fee unless we collect." This describes a contingency fee arrangement in which the lawyer's fee is contingent on (a percentage of) what you win and collect from the other party through a judgment or settlement. Lawyers who accept cases on a contingency fee basis accept a risk that you will win your case and that the losing party will have the money to pay up. Your state may regulate the maximum percentage a lawyer can accept under a contingency arrangement as well as the cases that cannot be handled on a contingency basis (such as criminal or divorce matters).

Contingency fee arrangements are not right for every matter. They are common in personal injury cases, or cases involving loss or damage to something of great value. Consequently, if you have a veterinary malpractice case based on the loss of your $1,500 horse, lawyers will likely reject this arrangement because the fee will not adequately compensate the lawyer for his or her time.

Contingency fee arrangements should always be put in writing. The written agreement should specify the percentage the lawyer will receive from your judgment or settlement. Keep in mind that these fee agreements usually make you reimburse the lawyer for his or her expenses and costs, such as witness fees, deposition transcripts, investigative fees, and many others.

Modified contingency fee. The modified contingency fee arrangement resembles the contingency fee agreement, described above. Through this arrangement, the lawyer charges a reduced hourly rate and bills you for each hour he or she spends on your matter, but if the case ends favorably for you, the lawyer will receive an additional sum of money.

Flat fee. If you want the lawyer to draft a basic equine-related contract, prepare a simple will, handle an uncontested divorce, or represent you in an uncomplicated case, the lawyer might be willing to work for a flat fee (one price only).

Paying the Lawyer In Advance

Under standard ethics rules, the client must pay the expenses in a legal action. Mindful of this, lawyers might ask you to pay in advance a sum of money that will cover expenses for filing fees, witness fees, subpoena costs, document retrieval costs, investigative fees, and others.

Before the legal work begins, typically in hourly fee arrangements, the lawyer may ask you to pay a sum of money called a "retainer fee." This amount often represents your advance payment of several hours of legal work.

For your protection, make sure that the retainer is combined with a written "retainer agreement" (discussed later in this section). Ethics rules usually forbid lawyers from immediately spending the retainer fee. Rather, lawyers usually must deposit the retainer funds into their attorney trust accounts, and only draw money from that account after services have actually been rendered and legal fees earned.

Getting the Arrangement in Writing

Particularly in ongoing matters (such as a lawsuit or a probate proceeding), or matters where a large fee is involved, both the client and the attorney benefit by having a written agreement that addresses the billing arrangement and the details of the representation. Retainer agreements often:

- Specify what services the lawyer will provide
- List the lawyer's rates for expenses chargeable to you (such as faxes, copies, telephone calls, mileage, paralegal work, express mailings and others)
- Acknowledge the lawyer's receipt of the retainer
- Explain the client's obligation (if any) to make further payment after the retainer is used up

It pays to read the retainer agreement *carefully* before you sign it, and make sure you agree with it. These agreements cover services, costs and refunds. For example, if your legal matter ends before your retainer fee has been used up, the retainer agreement might allow you a refund of the portion the lawyer did not earn. Or, the agreement might let the lawyer keep this money.

Is an Attorney Who Practices Equine Law Better Than One Who Does Not?

Not necessarily. In fact, if you already have an attorney-client relationship, and if you and your lawyer are confident that he or she can serve you well on your equine-related matter, you have found your lawyer.

The fact is, however, that the law has become very complex. More than ever, lawyers have become specialists in certain areas of the law. General practitioner lawyers, who handle a wide range of legal matters, may have no experience or understanding about matters involving horses. Your legal fees could be higher if you hire a lawyer who lacks equine law expertise. For example, the lawyer will need to spend more time researching the law and learning basic horse terminology. In most cases, *you* are paying that lawyer to learn.

Sometimes, it can benefit you to hire a lawyer experienced in equine law. These lawyers stand a better chance of having familiarity with your equine-related issues. Also, because people in the horse industry frequently have emergencies, lawyers who practice equine law are often well situated to help with prompt decision-making. For example:

- A boarding stable client might have a boarded horse, on which the stable usually has a lien, but the owner may be trying to haul it away. An equine lawyer will usually be able to spot the issue of the stablemen's lien law and tell, almost instantly, how it applies in this situation.

- A horse trainer could be faced with a colicky horse whose owner cannot be reached to consent to expensive colic surgery. The equine lawyer's understanding of horses and the law will help him or her better advise the trainer of how to fulfill his legal obligations.

- A riding instructor about to conduct a clinic in another state might wonder whether an equine liability law in that state obligates the instructor to post signs or update her contracts. An experienced equine lawyer will instantly know how to find the law—or may already have it—and provide prompt advice.

Because of their expertise, lawyers with equine law practices can, in many cases, save money because often they can get the work done in less time.

Conclusion

In conclusion, keep these ideas in mind:

1. Just because a lawyer purports to practice "equine law" does not necessarily mean that he or she is the best lawyer for you and your equine-related legal matter. Your matter might call for a tax specialist, criminal law specialist, or municipal law/zoning specialist. Make sure that you are comfortable with the lawyer, his or her level of experience, and rates.

2. Many lawyers allow free consultations, often over the phone, to allow you and the lawyer to evaluate each other and briefly discuss your legal matter. At the end of the consultation, the lawyer can explain whether he or she is interested in handling your matter and you can decide whether you want to hire the lawyer.

3. A lawyer's affiliation (or lack of affiliation) with a law firm tells little. What really matters is his or her ability, reputation, and capability of providing the type of assistance you seek at the price you are willing to pay.

How to Win Back Your Legal Fees
in a Legal Dispute

"I'll see you in court!" These were the forceful words of Harry, a disgruntled horse buyer. Harry recently spent $ 1,200 to buy a horse, only to find out that it was lame when he brought it home. There was no written contract. The seller refused to take back the horse or give Harry a refund, claiming that the horse was perfectly sound before it stepped foot in Harry's trailer.

Harry knows he has a case. His lawyer agrees. Why, then, was the lawyer so unwilling to handle the case? To reassure the lawyer, Harry even told him, "When I win the case, the other party will pay your legal fees." This seemed of no comfort to Harry's lawyer, either.

Is Harry correct? Is the losing party in a legal dispute always required pay the winning party's legal fees? The answer is "No."

Only under limited circumstances, generally described here, can a party in a lawsuit win back his or her legal fees. In the United States (as compared to England with its "loser pays" rule), each party must bear the cost of his or her own legal fees. Only four settings exist in which a court will order one party to pay the other's legal fees in a legal dispute.

1. The Parties Had an Enforceable, Written Contract That Specifically Covers Payment of Legal Fees

To increase your chances of winning back your legal fees in a lawsuit, use a carefully written contract from the start. Your contracts can clearly specify the settings in which you or the other party can win back your legal fees if the contract is breached (violated). Here is one example of how the contract can include this language:

Should either party breach this Agreement, the breaching party shall pay the other's court or arbitration costs and reasonable attorney's fees related to such breach.

13

If a dispute develops, you would ask the court to enforce this agreement. In Harry's situation, he had no written contract.

2. An Applicable Statute Provides for Attorney Fees

Some state and federal laws have language that awards a winning party his or her legal fees from the losing party in a legal dispute. Here are examples of some laws containing these provisions:

- Deceptive trade practice laws or consumer protection laws
- Civil rights and anti-discrimination laws
- Fair debt collection practice laws
- Antitrust laws

Depending on the law's language, your entitlement to win back legal fees can be automatic—all it takes is winning the case and proving that the losing party broke the law. In other cases, the law might require that you only stand to win back your legal fees if the court finds that the losing party "willfully" or intentionally broke the law. Laws with this language make it harder to win back your legal fees.

3. An Applicable Court Rule Provides for Payment of Legal Fees

Every court system has a written set of rules, called "court rules," that govern how lawsuits must proceed. In some instances, these rules give judges the discretion to order one party to pay some or all of the other's legal fees and costs when certain situations occur, such as:

- The losing party failed to show up in court to defend a lawsuit. (Lawyers call this non-appearance a "default.") In this setting, the winning party might be entitled to win back his or her legal fees, especially if the court finds sufficient proof that the non-appearing party had proper notice of the lawsuit and was aware of the need to appear in court.
- The court believes that one of the parties in the lawsuit disobeyed a valid order of the court.

4. The Court Specifically Found that the Other Party Asserted a "Frivolous" Claim or Defense in the Lawsuit

When a judge believes that a party has set forth a frivolous case or defense, or has somehow acted in "bad faith" throughout the lawsuit, the judge has the power to punish the wrongdoer. As an example of this punishment, the court can order the wrongdoer to pay the other

14

party's legal fees and court costs. However, courts are *very* unwilling to do this, as this author—despite 14 years of active law practice—has found.

Conclusion

In conclusion, please keep these ideas in mind:

1. If you have a legal dispute over a small amount of money, your legal fees might add up to more than the amount at stake. In these settings, people like Harry can handle their disputes without a lawyer in small claims courts. [See *Equine Law & Horse Sense* for more information on small claims courts.]

2. Sometimes it makes good economic sense to bypass the legal system altogether, especially where the amount at stake is small. Consider alternatives such as arbitration or community-based dispute resolution centers. *[Equine Law & Horse Sense* offers more information on these options.]

3. People involved in equine transactions should plan ahead with good contracts. An important detail in a contract is a clause that addresses who will pay the legal fees if a legal dispute arises. Or, the parties can agree *up front* in the contract to submit their disputes to binding arbitration or mediation. Waiting until a dispute arises is usually pointless.

4. Possibly, your legal expenses can be negotiated up front with your lawyer in an effort to contain them. This chapter explores several options for lowering your legal expenses.

5. Even if a court commands one party to pay the other's legal fees, certain factors can complicate the actual recovery of money. As one example, the other party might not have enough money to pay the fee. Or, the court might scrutinize the cost of the services or volume of work performed and only award reimbursement of some of the legal fees and not all. An appeal of a court's ruling could hold up the matter, and payment, for years.

FINDING A LAWYER AT LOW COST

You know you have a good case. A horse seller is refusing to refund your deposit of $2,500 on a horse you planned to buy. The purchase agreement you signed with the horse's seller required the seller to refund your deposit if the horse failed to X-ray clean during his pre-purchase exam. And fail he did. You want your $2,500 refund, but you realize that your legal fees will likely exceed this amount. Are other options available within your budget?

Yes. Low-cost legal services are available, if you qualify. Also, there are some money-saving alternatives to the legal system. If your funds are low, it pays to be aware of them. The notion of a "court-appointed" lawyer in every type of legal matter is a myth, as you will see. And not all legal disputes require extensive work from a lawyer, either. You might just hire a lawyer to write a simple demand letter in an attempt to resolve the dispute without undergoing costly legal proceedings.

What Makes Legal Services Costly?

Legal systems in other countries, such as Great Britain, impose a "loser pays" rule. In the United States, *you* usually bear the cost of your own legal fees. The few settings in which the loser pays were explained earlier in this Chapter.

Options to Resolve Your Dispute Without a Lawyer

You have a few options for handling a dispute on your own without a lawyer. Here are some of them:

Community dispute resolution or mediation centers. Your community, or one nearby, may have a community dispute resolution center or a neighborhood justice center. These are designed to help people quickly and inexpensively settle their differences. With the cooperation of both parties in a dispute, these centers can help schedule a meeting in which you and the other party can discuss the problem and how to resolve it. Depending on the center, they can provide offices and trained personnel to help the parties work constructively and positively. To find out about community dispute resolution or mediation centers in your area, contact your local courthouse, library, city hall, or state or local bar association.

Small claims court. Within every county are several small claims courts, although each state may give these courts a different name. These courts are set up to resolve disputes involving small amounts of money. The maximum amount of money within the jurisdiction of a small claims court varies from state to state. In California, Georgia, Pennsylvania, and Texas, people may seek up to $5,000 in a small claims court case. Tennessee allows recovery of up to $10,000 and in some instances $15,000. Michigan just increased its small claims court limit to $3,000. Small claims courts are usually designed for people to represent themselves without a lawyer.

Finding Low Cost Legal Services

Although you may have a legal right to receive a court-appointed and court-paid lawyer in some criminal matters, you do not have that right in a civil matter (civil matters involve money, as opposed to criminal law violations). If you qualify for free or low cost legal services, you have a few options, including:

Legal aid organizations. Legal aid programs provide free or reduced cost legal services to those who qualify. Eligibility varies, and you will be asked to give information about your income, living expenses, financial needs, and the size of your family. Check your phone book under the heading "Legal Aid" or "Legal Services," or contact your local courthouse.

Free legal clinics at local law schools. Many law schools offer legal-aid clinics, operated by the students, for people in their communities. These clinics typically help people with consumer legal problems, traffic tickets, landlord-tenant matters and simple matters. For more information, contact a law school in your area.

Other legal assistance programs. Bar associations (lawyer groups) in many states have organized special programs that offer low-cost legal services to people of limited means, who earn too much money to qualify for free legal aid, yet do not have the means to afford a lawyer at the usual rates. These programs are encouraged by the American Bar Association and are frequently known as "Greater Access to Justice Projects." To find out whether your state has a project, contact the American Bar Association [telephone number: (312) 988-5000, web site: www.aba.org/] or your state or local bar association.

A Lawyer as Your "Legal Coach" While You Do Most of the Work Yourself

Many of us in the horse industry have succeeded quite well as "do-it-yourselfers." Without anyone else's help, we often breed, raise, and train our own horses, and we handle our own business matters. When a legal matter arises, however, many of us continue this degree of self-reliance and try to do the work ourselves.

Before becoming a "do-it-yourself" lawyer, and handling a legal matter on your own through the court system, consider the possibility of hiring a lawyer for only a few hours' time. Your lawyer acts as a behind-the-scenes "coach" to give you direction and to help you succeed.

What is a "Legal Coach"

Lawyers typically do not see their role as a "legal coach." Rather, lawyers are usually hired to handle a matter completely, writing a contract or taking a case from start to finish through the court system. At your request, a lawyer might be willing to advise you while you do most of the work yourself, unless state ethics rules prevent this activity. This kind of arrangement can offer tremendous cost savings, but be aware that it is also riddled with potential risks.

Benefits of a "Legal Coach"

Here are some services a lawyer can provide on a limited or short-term basis:

Assessing the dollar value of a case. If you plan to represent yourself in a small claims court case, a lawyer can assess the facts and help you decide what sum of money the law entitles you to request from the other party.

Evaluating the merits of your case. Possibly, you are so devoted to your case that you cannot see its weaknesses. A lawyer can explain whether your position has a good chance of winning and is worth your time and effort.

Evaluating the merits of your defense. If somebody has been threatening you with legal action in a minor matter, and you are unsure whether to give in, settle the matter, or fight, a lawyer can offer direction.

Approving or "ghost writing" a demand letter. Possibly, you can write a simple demand letter to send to the other person or business to resolve your legal dispute. A lawyer can review the letter before you send it. Or, a lawyer can write it for you to sign, with no mention of the lawyer's name (this is commonly known as "ghost writing"). [*Equine Law & Horse Sense* covered how to write a demand letter.]

Provide court forms. When it comes to legal filings you give to the court in your case, sometimes better documents produce better results. A "legal coach" can help this effort.

Legal research and analysis. In some matters, such as a stablemen's lien foreclosure sale, the lawyer can research the law for you and tell you the measures you must take to legally comply with your state's law.

Secure experts. A lawyer can help you locate and hire expert witnesses that you might need to support your case.

Advise of alternatives to the court system. Alternatives to the traditional court system – such as mediation, arbitration, and small claims court – have become popular. [These alternatives were explained in *Equine Law & Horse Sense*.] A lawyer can advise you of which option, if any, makes sense for your matter and how you can pursue it on your own.

Help strengthen your in-court presentation. If you are representing yourself in a small claims court case, for example, a lawyer can help you develop a stronger in-court appearance. In this connection, the lawyer can offer suggestions for arguments you can present at trial or at important hearings.

Risks and Limitations of the "Legal Coach"

The "legal coach" concept has risks. Here are two of them:

State ethics restrictions . Bar association ethics rules in the applicable state might impair a lawyer's ability to represent clients who will do most of the legal work themselves.

Complex legal matters. Complex and high-dollar legal matters usually do not justify having a non-lawyer handle them, much less hiring a lawyer on a limited basis.

Confirming the Limited Engagement

If you request legal assistance on a limited basis, and if the lawyer agrees, the lawyer will likely ask you to sign a written agreement acknowledging the special arrangement. Possibly, if the lawyer is hired to draft court filings for you, such as your complaint or petition in a lawsuit, your state might require the lawyer to place his or her name directly on the court filing to affirm that he or she drafted it.

CHAPTER TWO

CONTRACTS AND HOW TO AVOID DISPUTES WITH THEM

Avoiding the Pitfalls that Create Disputes Involving an Equine-related Contract

Are you looking for ways to part with more of your hard-earned money and to create chaos in your life? Would you like to improve your chances of getting involved in a legal dispute? Of course not. I have listed six ways that people inadvertently create a contract dispute—and even more ways that you can easily avoid one.

Pitfall 1:　　　　**Doing business on a handshake, with nothing in writing**

How to Avoid:　　**Use a well-written contract**

Here are some of the reasons people have given for not using written contracts:

- "We are good friends, and we trust each other. Putting paperwork between us might cause suspicion or ill will."

- "Contracts are too expensive, especially because lawyers cost so much to write them."

- "We understand this sale and want to keep it simple. A contract would only complicate things."

In my 14 years as a practicing attorney, I have personally heard each of these reasons for not using a written contract. That is, I have heard them from people who later found themselves fighting a legal battle over their handshake deal. Since the beginning of time, most horse-related transactions have been done on a handshake, but that is not the safest way. Without a written contract, you may be vulnerable.

What are the benefits of a written contract? Here are a few:

- The written contract can offer a lasting reminder of what the parties intended, or as one author once put it, "paper does not tend to forget." For example, it will take a written contract to affirm whether or not a horse was sold "as is," with no promises or warranties as to its condition or usefulness.

- The mere process of entering into a contract tells a great deal about the other party's sincerity. For instance, if a horse seller swears that a horse has never taken a lame step or that a

23

broodmare is guaranteed to be fertile, he or she should put it in writing, if you so request.

- A contract (if it is written well enough to cover key elements of an arrangement fairly) can eliminate disputes completely, or, at a minimum, limit them to only a few issues. For instance, if two people had a written contract to lease a horse, but the contract does not say when their lease ends, then the contract would be helpful in narrowing any disputes to one issue—when does the lease end? Without the written contract, the parties might have battled over whether they even had a lease, or whether their deal was really a sale or even a gift.

Certainly, this does not mean that all verbal contracts are invalid. They can be valid in many instances. The problem is, legal disputes do happen. And when these disputes focus on a verbal contract, they often turn into a "shouting match" when each party to the very same transaction has a completely different understanding of the agreement. In a court of law, when these sharp differences take center stage, the question becomes whom to believe. As a result, the outcome can never be certain for anyone involved. One thing is guaranteed, however— the lawsuit *will* be expensive and time-consuming.

Pitfall 2:   **Losing the contract**

How to Avoid: **File the contract in a safe place**

Paperwork serves an important purpose. If a dispute later develops involving your agreement, the written contract is the first thing you will check. But what if you cannot find it? If you do not have the contract, you have no proof of the agreement or its details. For this reason, make sure to keep your contracts stored in a secure place. Do not discard them until after you are certain, or have confirmed with your lawyer, that the time frame for a legal dispute (called the "statute of limitations") has expired and that the contract is no longer needed.

Pitfall 3:   **Failing to have the contract properly signed where minors are involved**

How to Avoid: **Get the right adult involved in the contract**

Even the best-written contract risks failure if it has been improperly signed. In the horse industry, contracts involving minors (typically, people under the age of 18) are often signed improperly—and nobody knows it until they need the contract to work for them.

State laws generally prevent minors from entering into many types of contracts that do not involve the necessities of life. Horses, as important as they seem to be, do not legally qualify as "necessities of life" in the eyes of the law.

With this in mind, if you sell, train, or board horses with a minor, be sure *at least* one of his or her parents or legal guardians signs the contract. The signature of the minor's babysitter, next-door neighbor, friend, or non-parent relative is virtually guaranteed to be legally inadequate.

Pitfall 4:	**Assuming that contracts, such as releases or waivers of liability, are not worth the paper on which they are printed**
How to Avoid:	**Learn the facts**

Written contracts are usually binding, and releases of liability (also known as waivers) deserve your attention—regardless of whether you sign them or ask others to sign them. Releases of liability are enforceable in almost all 50 states. Most states will enforce these contracts, as long as they are worded and signed properly. Chapter Eight of this book discusses legal aspects of waivers and releases and what tends to make them fail. [*Equine Law & Horse Sense* covers 15 common characteristics of effective liability releases.]

Pitfall 5:	**Using form contracts without checking to see that they are legal or that they serve your needs.**
How to Avoid:	**Use forms only as a starting point**

Ready-to-use form contracts are cheap and quick. However, they run a risk of having illegal or unenforceable language or failing to include language your state law requires. In an installment sale contract, for example, buyers and sellers of horses typically have opposing interests from the moment the arrangement begins:

- *Horse buyers* often want to spread out their payments over time, and they like the grace periods (the extra time after the real due date in which the seller can receive a payment) to be as long as possible. If the horse should become unsuitable or unsound before the final payment is due, buyers often want to reserve the right to send back the horse for a full refund.

- *Horse sellers*, in sharp comparison, often want opposite things. They want the money to come in faster, for example, by shortening the payment schedule and by giving the buyer short (or no) grace periods. If the buyer should miss a payment, sellers typically want the right to re-possess a horse right away, without first going through the court system. Also, if an installment sale transaction fails, sellers often want to keep some or all of the buyer's installment money; this money, sellers may believe, compensates for the fact that the horse has been off the market from potential buyers, and may be less marketable.

Forms designed to be "one-size-fits all" sometimes fail to take into account certain important interests of the parties who rely on them; rather than account for these special interests, forms tend to ignore them altogether.

Forms can be a good start, when used properly. Many people – and almost all lawyers—have never before seen a horse-related contract. For them, the form is an example of what factors are generally important. The form offers a starting point from which to develop a customized contract that covers special interests and legal requirements.

Pitfall 6:	**Failing to pay attention to important details**
How to Avoid:	**Learn the details that make the difference in horse-related contracts**

Details really can make all the difference between a contract's success or failure. Read on in this chapter about 10 details that can be used in almost every horse-related contract.

Ten Important Details for Equine Contracts

Do your contracts account for the unique requirements of your state's law? The right contract language can help avoid disputes—and lower your expense if a dispute should arise. Details can separate marginal contracts from effective ones. Details can also help prevent legal disputes. Your effort to consider the right details will likely pay off in a savings of both money and aggravation.

Here are ten important, and often little known, details you should consider when developing your horse-related contracts. You can discuss with your lawyer which details are right for your situation.

1. Name the right parties
2. Name or describe the horse involved
3. Include Equine Activity Liability Act language
4. Pay attention to certain non-equine laws
5. Specify alternative ways to resolve disputes
6. Specify how the contract can be changed in the future
7. Confirm that the other party has authority to sign the contract
8. Consider indemnification language
9. Consider who will pay attorney fees, if a dispute arises
10. Make insurance part of the contract

1. Name the Right Parties

Whether they know it or not, many professionals in the horse industry do not properly sign their own contracts. This can happen, for instance, when a professional signs breeding contracts, boarding contracts, sales agreements, and property leases on behalf of an equine business, but neglects to name the business entity as the true party to the contract.

Here are some examples of how this problem can be prevented:

Assuming that the equine professional is a general partnership, the contracts can specify, for example:

Auspicious Show Horses,
a Missouri General Partnership

By: _____
    Gene A. Winner, General Partner
    On Behalf of the Partnership

If the professional is a corporation, the contract can specify:

Auspicious Show Horses, Inc.,
a California corporation

By: _____
    Gene A. Winner, President

By comparison, if the equine professional is a sole proprietor doing business under an assumed or fictitious name, the contract can state:

Sue Ellen Green, d/b/a Blue Ribbon Farms

By: _____
    Sue Ellen Green

Attention to these details can be critical factors in the validity of the contract. Not only will parties to the contract be better advised of the true identity of the other, but properly naming the business entity as a party to the contract can help avoid legal challenges against the business entity's individual proprietors, as explained in Chapter Five.

2. Name or Describe The Horse Involved

Everyone benefits if the contract specifies the horse involved. The contract can state the horse's registered name, barn name, sex, registration number and/or tattoo number, and markings. If a sales contract involves, for example, a mare that is certified to be carrying a foal sired by a particular stallion, the contract can specify the stallion and whether the mare's new owner is entitled to receive any return breeding privileges under a live foal guarantee.

3. Include Equine Activity Liability Act Language (Especially Where Required by Law)

Equine activity liability laws have created an important fine point for horse-related contracts. As of January 2000, 44 states have passed laws that are designed to affect liability involving equines and equine activities. Several of these laws require special language in certain equine-related contracts or releases. The state-by-state differences in the equine liability laws can be tremendous, as you will see as you read on in this Chapter to find the contract language requirements.

28

4. Pay Attention to Certain Non-Equine Laws

State laws sometimes affect, or create, many other details for contracts. Examples of some contract provisions affected by each state's law are:

Repossession. In an installment sale, horse sellers usually want to protect their right to repossess (take back) a horse if the buyer fails to make payment. In many states, laws address how - and if - a contract can legally allow the seller to repossess the horse without first getting approval from the proper court.

Interest on money owed. State laws specify the highest allowable interest rate that individuals or businesses can charge to those who owe them money. Whether they know it or not, many people use contracts that ask for unlawfully high rates of interest. When in doubt, your contract can always specify a rate of interest along with additional wording – for example: "7% or the highest rate of interest allowed under the law of this state, whichever is greater."

Stablemen's lien/agister's lien laws. An "agister's lien" (sometimes called a stablemen's lien) is much like a mechanic's lien. These liens occur when someone leaves a vehicle (in the setting of a mechanic's lien) or a horse (in the setting of a stablemen's lien/agister's lien) with someone for care and keeping. State laws govern when the keeper can sell the item to recover unpaid fees. These laws often provide that the item cannot be removed from the garage or stable until all fees are paid in full. The contract can affirm this law; or, it might benefit the stable to find out whether the law can be avoided through other language.

Sales or use tax. State laws may address sales or use taxes and who must pay them. Sales taxes apply to the retail sale of tangible personal property, which can include saddles, equipment, and horses. In most states, the seller collects sales tax from the buyer and remits it to the state. By comparison, use taxes can be imposed when someone buys personal property (such as a saddle) out-of-state but later brings it into the taxing state to be stored, used, or consumed. These taxes might affect sales, breeding, or lease contracts with horses. When in doubt, the contract can specify who should pay them.

Liability releases. Most states will enforce liability releases (also called "waivers") if they are properly presented and signed. What qualifies as proper language for these documents can vary widely from state to state. This chapter addresses some of these requirements (as of January 2000). To find other ways the law affects these documents, your lawyer can check court decisions from the applicable state.

Disclaimers of warranties in sales contracts. State laws (usually the state's commercial code) often specify how a seller can disclaim (cast aside) warranties in certain sales transactions. In the horse setting, the seller may want to disclaim a warranty of the horse's fitness for a particular purpose. Many states allow this, as long as the seller uses conspicuous (noticeable) language in the contract. Some state laws tell how the language must read. Below is one example of a disclaimer in a horse sale contract used in Kentucky many years ago:

> SELLER MAKES NO WARRANTIES, EITHER EXPRESS OR IMPLIED, AS TO THE SOUNDNESS, HEALTH, CONDITION, CONFORMATION, OR REPRODUCTIVE QUALITIES OF THE HORSE HEREBY SOLD AND SPECIFICALLY, BUT NOT ALL INCLUSIVELY, THERE IS NO EXPRESS OR IMPLIED WARRANTY OF MERCHANTABILITY OR FITNESS FOR A PARTICULAR PURPOSE, AND BUYER SHALL ACCEPT DELIVERY OF THE HORSE "AS IS." SELLER DOES HEREBY BIND ITSELF AND ITS SUCCESSORS AND ASSIGNS TO FOREVER WARRANT AND DEFEND THE TITLE TO THE AFORESAID PROPERTY UNTO THE SAID BUYER AND ITS SUCCESSORS AND ASSIGNS, AGAINST THE LAWFUL CLAIM OR CLAIMS OF ANY AND ALL PERSONS WHOMSOEVER.

This contract's use of capital letters was no accident. It was intended to set apart the disclaimer from the rest of the contract and draw the reader's attention to it.

5. Address Alternative Ways to Resolve Disputes

Resolving legal disputes through the court system can be time-consuming and costly. Alternative methods of resolving disputes, whether through arbitration or mediation, have become popular because they are generally considered quicker and cheaper than the court system. Once parties have become embroiled in a legal dispute, it is usually too late to find them agreeing on anything – much less agreeing to settle their differences through arbitration or mediation. Contracts, however, can protect the right to resolve certain matters through these methods. [NOTE: *Equine Law & Horse Sense* covers arbitration and mediation.]

With *arbitration*, the parties agree to have one or more arbitrators listen to both sides of a case, hear key witnesses, examine important documents, and then render a decision. The parties to the dispute usually agree from the start that the arbitrator's decision shall be valid and binding. Or, in some cases, the parties can agree that the arbitrator's decision will not be binding, and they will be free to continue their dispute through the court system.

Mediation is a process in which the parties to a dispute agree to allow one or more unbiased persons to help resolve it. Mediation differs from the traditional court system and the arbitration process. In those settings, a winner or loser emerges. The job of a mediator, however, is not to decide who wins or loses. Rather, the mediator encourages both sides to discuss their positions and to resolve their disputes. The mediation process is typically informal.

Despite their benefits, arbitration and mediation are not suitable for resolving every legal dispute. Some disputes are best handled through the court system, such as issues involving eviction in a landlord-tenant matter or stablemen's lien issues. Because of this, think carefully before agreeing to handle all disputes through these alternatives.

6. Specify How The Written Contract Can Be Changed in the Future

The last thing you can afford is for the other party to claim that your contract was somehow changed or even canceled through a *verbal agreement*, or that you had another verbal contract in effect beyond the written one. This can be prevented by making sure the contract addresses how the contract can be changed. To protect their integrity and to prevent a party from wrongly changing them, contracts can include statements such as:

- The parties intend for the written contract to be the complete expression of their understanding

- The written contract replaces any prior understandings that the parties may have had

- The written contract can only be modified or terminated by a written agreement that has been signed by all parties

7. Confirm That The Other Party Has Authority to Sign the Contract

If you are entering into a contract with someone who claims he is signing on behalf of someone else – such as the sales agent signing for the owner, or the person claiming to be signing on behalf of a corporation—how can you be sure that this person has the authority to act on behalf of a person or an entity?

With careful language in your contract, you can protect yourself in these settings. For example:

- Your contract can state that someone purporting to sign on behalf of a corporation or entity represents and affirms that he or she has authority to bind the entity and/or has been given proper

31

authority from the corporation to sign the contract and enter into the transaction at issue.

- Your contract can name the owner and specify that the sales agent, the one signing, has been approved to sign the contract for the owner. When in doubt, the safest option is to demand that the other person, the horse's owner, sign the contract, too.

8. Consider Indemnification Language

Indemnification is a fine point that can be appropriate in a wide variety of contracts. Indemnification, in its most basic sense, is an arrangement in which someone agrees to compensate another for an anticipated loss or liability. For example, an indemnification provision can state that if the owner of a horse gets sued because of the wrongful acts of a trainer, then the trainer will pay the owner's legal fees, liabilities, or judgments.

Indemnification language can be appropriate for equine leases. A lessor (the one who owns a horse but is allowing a "lessee" to use it, under a special arrangement), in particular, risks being named in a lawsuit if the leased horse injures someone else – even though the lessor might be miles away from his or her horse while the lessee is using it. An indemnification provision within an equine lease typically would require the lessee to protect the lessor in this type of situation.

9. Address Who Pays Attorney Fees if a Dispute Arises

With few exceptions, all of which are explained in Chapter One, the United States does not have an automatic "loser pay" system for legal disputes. However, contracts can try to change this by specifying who will pay legal fees and court costs should a dispute arise.

Contract provisions involving attorney fees vary widely. For example:

- Some contracts specify that if two parties in a contract get into a legal dispute involving something in the contract, the winning party will recover his or her legal fees from the losing party.

- Some contracts specify that the one who breaches (violates) the contract must pay the non-breaching party's legal fees. An example of this language can be found in Chapter One.

- Some contracts specify that the entitlement to recover legal fees exists regardless of whether the legal dispute proceeds to a judgment in the court system. Because well over 80 percent of legal disputes never proceed to trial, this language can be important.

- Some contracts specify that only one party is entitled to recover his or her legal fees from the other. For example, many boarding contracts contain clauses specifying that the stable will recover its attorney fees from the boarder if any legal dispute arises between them.

10. Make Insurance Part of the Contract

Insurance now exists for numerous horse-related activities and interests. Here are a few instances in which a contract can address insurance:

Leases. A lease can specify, for example, who is responsible for keeping the leased horse insured with liability, mortality, loss of use, or major medical and surgical insurance while the lease is in effect.

Boarding contracts. Stables can require customers to give the names of their horses' mortality insurance carriers as well as the insurers' emergency contact numbers. This makes the stable well-equipped to notify a horse's insurer if a horse becomes injured or ill, if the horse's owner is not available to do this.

Waivers/releases of liability. Some stables and equine professionals—acting on the assumption (right or wrong) that uninsured customers could be more likely to file a lawsuit against them after an injury occurs—require guests or customers to specify in the contracts that they have their own medical insurance.

HOW THE EQUINE ACTIVITY LIABILITY LAWS AFFECT CONTRACTS AND RELEASES OF LIABILITY

Across the country, contracts are changing, almost overnight, as a result of developments in the law. As of January 2000, 44 states have passed laws designed to, in some way, limit or control liabilities in the horse industry. Most of these laws, which are commonly known as "Equine Activity Liability Laws," require certain individuals, businesses, and professionals in the horse industry to include special language in various types of written contracts.

To find out which states' equine liability laws affect contracts in that state, take a look at the list below.

ALABAMA
Citation: Code of Alabama of 1975, Section 6-5-337
Year Law Took Effect: 1993

Whose Contracts Are Affected: An "equine professional" or an "equine activity sponsor" (see law for definitions).

Contracts for What Services Are Affected: Contracts "for the providing of professional services, instruction, or the rental of equipment or tack, whether or not the contract involves equine activities on or off of the location or site of the equine professional's or the equine activity sponsor's business."

Contract language to include: See below.

WARNING

Under Alabama law, an equine activity sponsor or equine professional is not liable for an injury to or the death of a participant in equine activities resulting from the inherent risks of equine activities, pursuant to the Equine Activities Liability Protection Act.

ALASKA

No known equine liability law in effect as of January 2000.

ARIZONA
Citation: Arizona Revised Statutes, Section 12-553
Year Law Took Effect: 1994

Whose Contracts Are Affected: Unclear, possibly everyone's contracts.

Contracts for What Services/Language to Include: Arizona's equine liability law is less specific than other states regarding language to include in equine-related contracts. The law states, in part, that immunities apply when the participant (or a parent or legal guardian if the participant is under the age of 18) signs a release of liability "before taking control of the equine." The law also says:

> "A signed release acknowledges that the person is aware of the inherent risks associated with equine activities, is willing and able to accept full responsibilities for his own safety and welfare and releases the equine owner or agent from liability unless the equine owner or agent is grossly negligent or commits wilful, wanton or intentional acts or omissions."

Consequently, Arizona's law appears to suggest that liability releases may:

- List several inherent risks associated with equine activities
- Acknowledge that the signer is aware of the inherent risks
- Mention that the signer is willing and able to accept full responsibilities for his or her own safety and welfare
- Specify that the signer is releasing the equine owner or agent (or others affiliated with them) from liability unless the owner or agent is grossly negligent or commits wilful, wanton, or intentional acts or omissions. Your lawyer can advise you how to draft this in a legally-appropriate way

ARKANSAS
Citation: Arkansas Code of 1987,
**   Chapter 120, Section 16-120-201**
Year Law Took Effect: 1995

Whose Contracts Are Affected: The law does not appear to specify certain language to include in contracts.

CALIFORNIA

No known equine liability law in effect as of January 2000.

COLORADO
Citation: Colorado Revised Statutes, Section 13-21-119
Year Law Took Effect: 1990

Whose Contracts Are Affected: "Equine professionals" (see law for definitions).

Contracts for What Services Are Affected: Contracts "for the providing of professional services, instruction, or the rental of equipment or tack or an equine to a participant, whether or not the contract involves equine activities on or off of the location or site of the equine professional's business."

Contract Language to Include: See below.

WARNING

Under Colorado Law, an equine professional is not liable for an injury to or the death of a participant in equine activities resulting from the inherent risks of equine activities, pursuant to section 13-21-119, Colorado Revised Statutes.

CONNECTICUT
Citation: Connecticut General Statutes Annotated,
Section 52-557 p
Year Law Took Effect: 1993

Whose Contracts/Contracts For What Services Are Affected: The Connecticut statute involving assumption of risk in equine activities does not specify certain language to include in contracts. At a minimum, this law seems to invite the use of documents that require equine activity participants to acknowledge risks of engaging in equine activities.

DELAWARE
Citation: 1995 Delaware Code, Title 10,
Chapter 81, Section 8140
Year Law Took Effect: 1995

Whose Contracts Are Affected: "Equine professionals" (see law for definitions).

Contracts for What Services Are Affected: Contracts for "the providing of professional services, instruction, or the rental of equipment or tack or an equine to a participant, whether or not the contract involves equine activities on or off of the location or site of the equine professional's business."

Contract Language to Include: See below.

WARNING

Under Delaware Law, an equine professional is not liable for an injury to or the death of a participant in equine activities resulting from the inherent risks of equine activities, pursuant to 10 Delaware Code Section 8140.

FLORIDA
Citation: 1993 Florida Laws
          Chapter 93-169, Section773.01
Year Law Took Effect: 1993

Whose Contracts Are Affected: "Every equine activity sponsor and equine professional" (see law for definitions).

Contract Language to Include: See below.

WARNING

Under Florida law, an equine sponsor or equine professional is not liable for an injury to, or the death of, a participant in equine activities resulting from the inherent risks of equine activities.

The sign posting requirement, according to the Florida law, is relieved if the professional or equine activity sponsor complies with the above language requirement for contracts.

GEORGIA
Citation: Code of Georgia Annotated, Section 62-2701
Year Law Took Effect: 1991

Whose Contracts Are Affected: "An equine professional or an equine activity sponsor" (see law for definitions).

Contracts for What Services Are Affected: Contracts for "the providing of professional services, instruction, or the rental of equipment or tack or an equine to a participant, whether or not the contract involves equine activities on or off of the location or site of the equine professional's or the equine activity sponsor's business."

Contract Language to Include: See below.

> **WARNING**
>
> Under Georgia law, an equine activity sponsor or equine professional is not liable for an injury to or the death of a participant in equine activities resulting from the inherent risks of equine activities, pursuant to Chapter 12 of Title 4 of the Official Code of Georgia Annotated.

HAWAII
Citation: 1994 Hawaii A.L.S. 249
Year Law Took Effect: 1994

Whose Contracts/Contracts For What Services Are Affected: Hawaii's equine liability law (as of January 2000) does not appear to specify certain language to include in contracts.

IDAHO
Citation: Idaho Code of 1990, Chapter 18, Section 6-1801
Year Law Took Effect: 1990

Whose Contracts/Contracts For What Services Are Affected: Idaho's equine liability law (as of January 2000) does not appear to specify certain language to include in contracts.

ILLINOIS
Citation: 745 Illinois Statutes Annotated, Section 47/1
Year Law Took Effect: 1995

Whose Contracts Are Affected: "Equine professionals" (see law for definitions).

Contracts for What Services Are Affected: Contracts for "the providing of professional services, instruction, or the rental of equipment or tack or an equine to a participant, whether or not the contract involves equine activities on or off of the location or site of the equine professional's business."

Contract Language to Include: See below.

> **WARNING**
>
> Under the Equine Activity Liability Act, each participant who engages in an equine activity expressly assumes the risks of engaging in and legal responsibility for injury, loss, or damage to person or property resulting from the risk of equine activities.

Also, as to releases of liability, the Illinois law states:

"Each participant, or parent or guardian of a minor participant, may execute a release assuming responsibility for the risks of engaging in equine activities. The release shall give notice to the participant, or parent or guardian, of the risks of engaging in equine activities, including (i) the propensity of an equine to behave in dangerous ways that may result in injury to the participant, (ii) the inability to predict an equine's reaction to sound, movements, objects, persons, or animals, and (iii) the hazards of surface or subsurface conditions. A release shall remain valid until expressly revoked by a participant, or, if a minor, the parent or guardian."

This language suggests that liability releases in Illinois should, *at a minimum*, list the risks that are specified in the law.

INDIANA
Citation: Indiana Statutes Annotated, Section 34-31-5-1
Year Law Took Effect: 1995

Whose Contracts Are Affected: "Equine professionals" (see law for definitions).

Contracts for What Services Are Affected: Contracts for "the providing of professional services, providing of instruction, or rental of equipment or tack or an equine to a participant, whether or not the contract involves equine activities on or off of the location or site of the equine professional's business."

Contract Language to Include: See below.

WARNING

Under Indiana law, an equine professional is not liable for an injury to, or the death of, a participant in equine activities resulting from the inherent risks of equine activities.

IOWA
Citation: Iowa Code Annotated, Section 673.1
Year Law Took Effect: 1997

Whose Contracts Are Affected: "Domesticated animal professionals" (see law for definitions).

Contracts for What Services Are Affected: Contracts for "domesticated animal activities" (see law for definitions).

Contract Language to Include: See next page.

> WARNING
>
> UNDER IOWA LAW, A DOMESTICATED ANIMAL PROFESSIONAL IS NOT LIABLE FOR DAMAGES SUFFERED BY, AN INJURY TO, OR THE DEATH OF A PARTICIPANT RESULTING FROM THE INHERENT RISKS OF DOMESTICATED ANIMAL ACTIVITIES, PURSUANT TO IOWA CODE CHAPTER 673. YOU ARE ASSUMING INHERENT RISKS OF PARTICIPATING IN THIS DOMESTICATED ANIMAL ACTIVITY.

By all indications from the statute, the warning language cited above should be printed in capital letters. Also, the Iowa law requires inclusion of the following disclaimer in contracts:

> A number of inherent risks are associated with a domesticated animal activity. A domesticated animal may behave in a manner that results in damages to property or an injury or death to a person. Risks associated with the activity may include injuries caused by bucking, biting, stumbling, rearing, trampling, scratching, pecking, falling, or butting.
>
> The domesticated animal may act unpredictably to conditions, including, but not limited to, a sudden movement, loud noise, an unfamiliar environment, or the introduction of unfamiliar persons, animals, or objects.
>
> The domesticated animal may also react in a dangerous manner when a condition or treatment is considered hazardous to the welfare of the animal; a collision occurs with an object or animal; or a participant fails to exercise reasonable care, take adequate precautions, or use adequate control when engaging in a domesticated animal activity, including failing to maintain reasonable control of the animal or failing to act in a manner consistent with the person's abilities.

This language suggests that liability releases in Iowa should, *at a minimum*, list the "inherent risks" that are specified in the law.

KANSAS
Citation: 1994 Kansas A.L.S. 290
Year Law Took Effect: 1994

Whose Contracts Are Affected: "Domestic animal professionals" (see law for definitions).

Contracts for What Services Are Affected: Contracts for "the providing of professional services, instruction or the rental of equipment or tack or a domestic animal to a participant, whether or not the contract involves domestic animal activities on or off the location or site of the domestic animal professional's business."

Contract Language to Include: See below.

WARNING

Under Kansas law, there is no liability for an injury to or the death of a participant in domestic animal activities resulting from the inherent risks of domestic animal activities, pursuant to sections 1 through 4. You are assuming the risk of participating in this domestic animal activity.

Also, the Kansas statute also appears to require that "domestic animal professionals" include of the following language in their contracts:

Inherent risks of domestic animal activities include, but shall not be limited to:

(1) The propensity of a domestic animal to behave in ways i.e., running, bucking, biting, kicking, shying, stumbling, rearing, falling or stepping on, that may result in an injury, harm or death to persons on or around them;

(2) the unpredictability of a domestic animal's reaction to such things as sounds, sudden movement and unfamiliar objects, persons, or other animals;

(3) certain hazards such as surface and subsurface conditions;

(4) collisions with other domestic animals or objects; and

(5) the potential of a participant to act in a negligent manner that may contribute to injury to the participant or others, such as failing to maintain control over the domestic animal or not acting within such participant's ability.

This language suggests that liability releases used by "domestic animal professionals" in Kansas should, *at a minimum*, list the 5 "inherent risks" that are specified in that state's law.

KENTUCKY
Citation: Kentucky Revised Statutes, Section 247.401
Year Law Took Effect: 1996

Whose Contracts Are Affected: "Farm animal professionals" or "farm animal activity sponsors" (see law for definitions).

Contracts for What Services Are Affected: Contracts for "the providing of professional services, instruction, or the rental of equipment or tack or a farm animal to a participant, whether or not the contract involves farm animal activities on or off of the location or site of the farm animal professional's or farm animal activity sponsor's business."

Contract Language to Include: See below.

WARNING

Under Kentucky law, a farm animal activity sponsor, farm animal professional, or other person does not have the duty to eliminate all risks of injury of participation in farm animal activities. There are inherent risks of injury that you voluntarily accept if you participate in farm animal activities.

LOUISIANA
Citation: Louisiana Revised Statutes, Section 9:2795.1
Year Law Took Effect: 1992

Whose Contracts Are Affected: "Equine professionals" and "equine activity sponsors" (see law for definitions).

Contracts for What Services Are Affected: Contracts for "the provision of professional services, instruction, or the rental of equipment or tack or an equine to a participant, whether or not the contract involves equine activities on or off of the location or site of the equine professional's or the equine activity sponsor's business."

Contract Language to Include: See below.

WARNING

Under Louisiana law, an equine activity sponsor or equine professional is not liable for an injury to or the death of a participant in equine activities resulting from the inherent risks of equine activities, pursuant to R.S. 9:2795.1.1.

MAINE
Citation: Maine Statutes, Title 7, Section 4101
Year Law Took Effect: 1992

Whose Contracts Are Affected/Contracts for What Services Are Affected: Unclear.

Contract Language to Include: The Maine statute, amended in 1999, states that notice of inherent risks may be satisfied either by the posting of a proper sign or by a statement signed by the participant containing "at least" the following:

WARNING

UNDER MAINE LAW, AN EQUINE PROFESSIONAL HAS LIM-
ITED LIABILITY FOR AN INJURY OR DEATH RESULTING FROM
THE INHERENT RISKS OF EQUINE ACTIVITIES.

MARYLAND

No known equine liability law in effect as of January 2000.

MASSACHUSETTS
Citation: Massachusetts General Laws 128, Section 2D
Year Law Took Effect: 1992

Whose Contracts Are Affected: "Equine professionals" and "equine activity sponsors" (see law for definitions).

Contracts for What Services Are Affected: Contracts for "the provision of professional services, instruction, or the rental of equipment or tack or an equine to a participant, whether or not the contract involves equine activities on or off of the location or site of the equine professional's or the equine activity sponsor's business."

Contract Language to Include: See below.

WARNING

Under Massachusetts law, an equine professional is not liable for an injury to, or the death of, a participant in equine
activities resulting from the inherent risks of equine activities, pursuant to section 2D of chapter 128 of the General Laws.

MICHIGAN
Citation: Michigan Compiled Laws, Section 691.1661
Year Law Took Effect: 1995

Whose Contracts Are Affected: "Equine professionals" (see law for definitions).

Contracts for What Services Are Affected: Contracts for "providing professional services, instruction, or rental of equipment, tack, or an equine to a participant, whether or not the contract involves an equine activity on or off the location or site of the equine professional's business."

Contract Language to Include: See on next page.

> WARNING
>
> Under the Michigan equine activity liability act, an equine professional is not liable for an injury to or the death of a participant in an equine activity resulting from an inherent risk of the equine activity.

MINNESOTA
**Citation: Minnesota Statutes,
         Chapter 623, Article 3, Section 2**
Year Law Took Effect: 1994

Whose Contracts/Contracts For What Services Are Affected: Minnesota's equine liability law (as of January 2000) does not appear to specify certain language to include in contracts.

MISSOURI
Citation: Missouri Revised Statutes, Section 537.325
Year Law Took Effect: 1994

Whose Contracts Are Affected: "Equine professionals" and "equine activity sponsors" (see law for definitions).

Contracts for What Services Are Affected: Contracts for "the providing of professional services, instruction, or the rental of equipment or tack or an equine to a participant, whether or not the contract involves equine activities on or off of the location or site of the equine professional's or equine activity sponsor's business."

Contract Language to Include: See below.

> WARNING
>
> Under Missouri law, an equine professional is not liable for an injury to or the death of a participant in equine activities resulting from the inherent risks of equine activities pursuant to the Revised Statutes of Missouri.

MISSISSIPPI
Citation: Mississippi Code Annotated, Section 95-11-1
Year Law Took Effect: 1994

Whose Contracts Are Affected: "Equine professionals" and "equine activity sponsors" (see law for definitions).

Contracts for What Services Are Affected: Contracts for "the providing of professional services, instruction or the rental of equipment or tack, or an equine to a participant, whether or not the contract involves equine activities on or off of the location or site of the equine activity sponsor's or equine professional's business."

Contract Language to Include: See below.

WARNING:

Under Mississippi law, an equine activity or equine sponsor is not liable for an injury to or the death of a participant in equine activities resulting from the inherent risks of equine activities, pursuant to this chapter.

MONTANA
Citation: Montana Code Annotated, Section 27-1-725
Year Law Took Effect: 1993

Whose Contracts/Contracts For What Services Are Affected: Montana's equine liability law (as of January 2000) does not appear to specify certain language for contracts.

NEBRASKA
Citation: Revised Statutes of Nebraska, Section 25-21, 249
Year Law Took Effect: 1997

Whose Contracts Are Affected: "Equine professionals" (see law for definitions).

Contracts for What Services Are Affected: Contracts for "providing professional services, instruction, or rental of equipment or tack or an equine to a participant, whether or not the contract involves equine activities on or off the location or site of the equine professional's business."

Contract Language to Include: See below.

WARNING

Under Nebraska Law, an equine professional is not liable for an injury to or the death of a participant in equine activities resulting from the inherent risks of equine activities, pursuant to sections 25-21,249 to 25-21,253.

NEVADA

No known equine liability law in effect as of January 2000.

NEW HAMPSHIRE
Citation: New Hampshire Revised Statutes Annotated,
Section 508:19
Year Law Took Effect: 1999

Whose Contracts/Contracts For What Services Are Affected:
New Hampshire's equine liability law (as of January 2000) does not appear to specify certain language for contracts.

NEW JERSEY
Citation: New Jersey Statutes, 5:15-1
Year Law Took Effect: 1998

Whose Contracts/Contracts For What Services Are Affected:
New Jersey's equine liability law (as of January 2000) does not appear to specify certain language for contracts.

NEW MEXICO
Citation: New Mexico Statutes Annotated, Article 13,
Section 42-13-1
Year Law Took Effect: 1993

Whose Contracts/Contracts For What Services Are Affected:
New Mexico's equine liability law (as of January 2000) does not does not appear to specify certain language for contracts.

NEW YORK

No known equine liability law in effect as of January 2000.

NORTH CAROLINA
Citation: General Statutes of North Carolina,
Chapter 99E, Article 1
Year Law Took Effect: 1998

Whose Contracts Are Affected: "Equine professionals" and "equine activity sponsors" (see law for definitions).

Contracts for What Services Are Affected: Contracts for "the providing of professional services, instruction, or the rental of equipment or tack or an equine to a participant, whether or not the contract involves equine activities on or off the location or site of the equine professional's or the equine activity sponsor's business."

Contract Language to Include: See below.

WARNING

Under North Carolina law, an equine activity sponsor or equine professional is not liable for an injury to or the death of a participant in equine activities resulting exclusively from the inherent risks of equine activities. Chapter 99E of the North Carolina General Statutes.

NORTH DAKOTA
Citation: North Dakota Code, Section 53-10-1
Year Law Took Effect: 1991

Whose Contracts/Contracts For What Services Are Affected:
North Dakota's equine liability law (as of January 2000) does not appear to specify certain language for contracts.

OHIO
Citation: Ohio Revised Code, Section 2305.32.1
Year Law Took Effect: 1997

Whose Contracts Are Affected/Contracts for What Services Are Affected: Unclear, possibly everyone's contracts.

Contract Language to Include: The Ohio statute does not include a "warning" statement found in many other state laws but appears to contain these requirements geared to waivers:

> "A valid waiver for purposes of ... this Section shall be in writing and subscribed by the equine activity participant or the parent, guardian, custodian, or other legal representative of the equine activity participant, and shall specify at least each inherent risk of an equine activity that is listed [as cited below] ... and that will be a subject of the waiver of tort or other civil liability."

Also, the Ohio law appears to require the following language in waivers:

'Inherent risk of an equine activity' means a danger or condition that is an integral part of an equine activity, including, but not limited to, any of the following:

(a) The propensity of an equine to behave in ways that may result in injury, death, or loss to persons on or around the equine;

(b) The unpredictability of an equine's reaction to sounds, sudden movement, unfamiliar objects, persons, or other animals;

(c) Hazards, including, but not limited to, surface or subsurface conditions;

(d) A collision with another equine, another animal, a person, or an object;

(e) The potential of an equine activity participant to act in a negligent manner that may contribute to injury, death, or loss to the person of the participant or to other persons, including but not limited to, failing to maintain control over an equine or failing to act within the ability of the participant.

The boxed language on the previous page suggests that liability releases in Ohio should, *at a minimum*, list the 5 "inherent risks" that are specified in the law.

OKLAHOMA
Citation: Oklahoma Statutes, Title 76, Section 50.1
Year Law Took Effect: 1999

Whose Contracts/Contracts For What Services Are Affected/ Language: Oklahoma's equine liability law does not specify language nor does it single out contracts used by any particular segment of the equine industry. It states that " [t]wo or more persons may agree, in writing, to extend the waiver of liability pursuant to the provisions of the Oklahoma Livestock Activities Liability Limitation Act. Such waiver shall be valid and binding by its terms."

OREGON
Citation: Oregon Revised Statutes, Section 30.687
Year Law Took Effect: 1991

Whose Contracts Are Affected: "Equine professionals," "equine activity sponsors," and possibly others (see law for definitions).

Contracts for What Services Are Affected/Contract Language to Include: The Oregon statute does not require the "warning" statement found in many other state equine liability laws. However, the law appears to include certain requirements geared to liability releases and contracts presented in that state. The Oregon law, by its terms, provides that liability releases apply to *adult* participants. As to language for releases, the law states:

> "The limitations on liability provided in ORS 30.691 shall apply to an adult participant in the circumstances listed in subsection (1)(b) of this section if the participant, prior to riding, training, driving, grooming or riding as a passenger upon an equine, knowingly executes a release stating that as a condition of participation, the participant waives the right to bring an action against the equine professional or equine activity sponsor for any injury or death arising out of riding, training, driving, grooming or riding as a passenger upon the equine. A release so executed shall be binding upon the adult participant ...."

PENNSYLVANIA

No known equine liability law in effect as of January 2000.

RHODE ISLAND
Citation: Rhode Island Laws, Chapter 21, Section 4-21-1
Year Law Took Effect: 1993

Whose Contracts Are Affected: "Equine professionals" (see law for definitions).

Contracts for What Services Are Affected: Contracts for "the providing of professional services, instruction, or the rental of equipment or tack or an equine to a participant, whether or not the contract involves equine activities on or off the location or site of the equine professional's business."

Contract Language to Include: See below.

WARNING

Under Rhode Island Law, an equine professional, unless he or she can be shown to have failed to be in the exercise of due care, is not liable for an injury to, or the death of, a participant in equine activities resulting from the inherent risks of equine activities, pursuant to this chapter.

SOUTH CAROLINA
Citation: South Carolina Laws, Section 47-9-710
Year Law Took Effect: 1993

Whose Contracts Are Affected: "Equine professionals" and equine activity sponsors" (see law for definitions).

Contracts for What Services Are Affected: Contracts for "providing professional services, instruction, or rental of equipment, tack, or an equine to a participant, whether or not the contract involves equine activities on or off of the location or site of the business of the equine professional or equine activity sponsor."

Contract Language to Include: See below.

WARNING

Under South Carolina law, an equine activity sponsor or equine professional is not liable for an injury to or the death of a participant in an equine activity resulting from an inherent risk of equine activity, pursuant to Article 7, Chapter 9 of Title 47, Code of Laws of South Carolina, 1976.

SOUTH DAKOTA
Citation: South Dakota Laws Annotated, Section 42-11-1
Year Law Took Effect: 1993

Whose Contracts Are Affected: "Equine professionals" (see law for definitions).

Contracts for What Services Are Affected: Contracts for "the providing of professional services, instruction, or the rental of equipment or tack or an equine to a participant, whether or not the contract involves equine activities on or off of the location or site of the equine professional's business."

Contract Language to Include: See below.

WARNING

Under South Dakota law, an equine professional is not liable for an injury to or the death of a participant in equine activities resulting from the inherent risks of equine activities, pursuant to Section 42-11-2.

TENNESSEE
Citation: Tennessee Code Annotated, Section 44-20-101
Year Law Took Effect: 1992

Whose Contracts Are Affected: "Equine professionals" (see law for definitions).

Contracts for What Services Are Affected: Contracts for "providing of professional services, instruction, or the rental of equipment or tack or an equine to a participant, whether or not the contract involves equine activities on or off the location or site of the equine professional's business."

Contract Language to Include: See below.

WARNING

Under Tennessee Law, an equine professional is not liable for an injury to or death of a participant in equine activities resulting from the inherent risks of equine activities, pursuant to Tennessee Code Annotated, title 44, chapter 20.

TEXAS
Citation: Texas Code Annotated, Section 87.001
Year Law Took Effect: 1995

Whose Contracts Are Affected: "Equine professionals" (see law for definitions).

Contracts for What Services Are Affected: Contracts for "professional services, instruction, or the rental of equipment or tack or an equine animal. The language must be included in contracts without regard to whether the contract involves equine activities on or off the location or site of the business of the equine professional."

Contract Language to Include: See below.

WARNING

UNDER TEXAS LAW (CHAPTER 87, CIVIL PRACTICE AND REMEDIES CODE), AN EQUINE PROFESSIONAL IS NOT LIABLE FOR AN INJURY TO OR THE DEATH OF A PARTICIPANT IN EQUINE ACTIVITIES RESULTING FROM THE INHERENT RISKS OF EQUINE ACTIVITIES.

By all indications in the Texas statute, the warning language cited above should be in capital letters.

UTAH
Citation: Utah Code Annotated, Section 78-27b-101
Year Law Took Effect: 1992

Whose Contracts/Contracts For What Services Are Affected: Utah's equine liability law (as of January 2000) does not appear to specify certain language for contracts.

VERMONT
Citation: 12 Vermont Statutes Annotated, Section 1039
Year Law Took Effect: 1996

Whose Contracts Are Affected: "Equine activity sponsors" (see law for definitions).

Contracts for What Services Are Affected: Contracts for "providing of professional services, instruction, or rental of equipment or tack or an equine to a participant, whether or not the contract involves equine activities on or off the location or site of the equine professional's business."

Contract Language to Include: See next page.

WARNING

Under Vermont Law, an equine activity sponsor is not liable for an injury to, or the death of, a participant in equine activities resulting from the inherent risks of equine activities that are obvious and necessary, pursuant to 12 V.S.A § 1039.

VIRGINIA
Citation: Virginia Code, Chapter 27.5,
     Section 3.1-796.130
Year Law Took Effect: 1991

 Whose Contracts Are Affected/Contracts for What Services Are Affected/Contract Language to Include: Compared to other states, Virginia's equine liability law is less specific regarding language to include in equine-related contracts and releases. The Virginia law states:

> "The waiver shall give notice to the participant of the risks inherent in equine activities, including (i) the propensity of an equine to behave in dangerous ways which may result in injury to the participant; (ii) the inability to predict an equine's reaction to sound, movements, objects, persons, or animals; and (iii) hazards of surface or subsurface conditions."

This language suggests that liability releases/waivers in Virginia should, *at a minimum*, list the 3 inherent risks that are specified in the law.

WASHINGTON
Citation: Washington Revised Code, Section 4.24.530
Year Law Took Effect: 1989

 Whose Contracts/Contracts For What Services Are Affected: Washington's equine liability law (as of January 2000) does not appear to specify certain language for contracts.

WEST VIRGINIA
Citation: West Virginia Code, Article 4, Section 20-4-1
Year Law Took Effect: 1990

 Whose Contracts Are Affected/Contracts for What Services Are Affected/Contract Language to Include: The West Virginia law, compared to those of other states, is less specific regarding language to include in equine-related contracts. The West Virginia law states:

"Every horseman shall ... [p]repare and present to each participant or prospective participant, for his or her inspection and signature, a statement which clearly and concisely explains the liability limitations, restrictions and responsibilities set forth in this article."

The law lists several duties that are assumed by participants in equine activities. Consequently, West Virginia's law appears to suggest that equine activity participants should sign a statement that addresses, *at a minimum*, the following:

- Acknowledges that equestrian and other equine-related activities are hazardous to participants, regardless of all feasible safety measures which can be taken.

- Acknowledges that the signer expressly assumes the risk of and legal responsibility for any injury, loss or damage to person or property which results from participation in an equestrian activity.

- Acknowledges that each participant has the sole individual responsibility for knowing the range of his or her own ability to manage, care for, and control a particular horse or perform a particular equestrian activity.

- Affirms that it shall be the duty of each participant to act within the limits his or her own ability, to maintain reasonable control of the particular horse or horses at all times while participating in an equestrian activity, to heed all posted warnings, to perform equestrian activities only in an area or in facilities designated by the horseman and to refrain from acting in a manner which may cause or contribute to the injury of anyone.

- Agrees to accept full responsibility for a collision or fall and to release the equine professional, equine activity sponsor, and appropriately named persons or entities.

- Agrees that if the participant is involved in an accident, he or she shall not depart from the area or facility where the equestrian activity took place without leaving personal identification, including name and address, or without notifying the proper authorities, or without obtaining assistance.

WISCONSIN
Citation: Wisconsin Statutes Annotated, Section 895.481
Year Law Took Effect: 1996

Whose Contracts Are Affected: "Equine professionals" (see law for definitions).

53

Contracts for What Services Are Affected: Contracts for "the rental of equines or equine equipment or tack or for the instruction of a person in the riding, driving, or being a passenger upon an equine."

Contract Language to Include: See below.

NOTICE: A person who is engaged for compensation in the rental of equines or equine equipment or tack or in the instruction of a person in the riding or driving of an equine or in being a passenger upon an equine is not liable for the injury or death of a person involved in equine activities resulting from the inherent risks of equine activities, as defined in section 895.481(1)(e) of the Wisconsin Statutes.

The Wisconsin law specifies that the above warning language should be in clearly readable **bold** print of not less than the same size as the print used in the remainder of the contract.

WYOMING
Citation: Wyoming Statutes, Section 1-1-122
Year Law Took Effect: 1996

Whose Contracts/Contracts For What Services Are Affected: Wyoming's equine liability law (as of January 2000) does not appear to specify certain language for contracts.

Proper Compliance
With an Equine Activity Liability Law

Compliance with an equine liability law's contract language requirements can be very important. A small number of the laws have language that *expressly* conditions the entitlement to immunities on compliance with the sign and warning language requirements in the law. Laws with these provisions are presently found in Alabama, Georgia, Indiana, Kentucky, Louisiana, Mississippi, North Carolina, and South Carolina, but this is not meant to be an exhaustive list. Make sure to carefully read each equine liability law that applies where you do business and where you reside.

CHAPTER THREE

EQUINE SALES DISPUTES AND HOW TO AVOID THEM

PAPERS, PAPERS—WHO HAS THE PAPERS?
HOW TO AVOID DISPUTES ABOUT REGISTRATION PAPERS

Two months ago Jim bought the horse he always wanted. His goal was to win championships in breed-recognized horse shows. Now, however, a terrible problem has ended his plans: The seller refuses to transfer the horse's breed registration papers into Jim's name.

Jim's arsenal of weapons against the seller is limited—he has no written sales contract, but he recalls the seller promising to send him the horse's papers "right away" the day Jim paid for the horse (a promise the seller now denies ever making).

This section discusses some of a horse buyer's legal options when a seller fails to give breed registration papers, as well as how to avoid registration paper disputes.

The Buyer's Legal Options
When the Seller Fails to Transfer Papers

In the scenario above, the law gives Jim the buyer a few options in response to this problem. Unfortunately, none of them will be easy, and none will be cheap.

1. Sue the seller to fulfill (or, in legal terminology, to "specifically perform") his promise to transfer the horse's breed registration papers into your name as buyer.

When the seller fails to transfer the horse's registration papers into the buyer's name, the buyer can bring a claim of "specific performance." A legal action for "specific performance" asks the court to order a person, or business entity, to take a specific action. As easy as that may sound, lawsuits for specific performance can be very complex. In the example above, if Jim wants to succeed in his claim for specific performance, he would have to prove at least two things:

- The horse is unique, and only with the registration papers transferred into in Jim the buyer's name will it have value; and

- No other legal remedy, aside from getting the registration papers in Jim's name, will adequately compensate Jim in this situation.

The sad fact is, if the seller has no breed registration papers and cannot transfer them, buyers like Jim must resort to other legal options, such as those described below.

2. Sue the seller to rescind (nullify) the sale, take back the horse, and compensate the buyer for all out of pocket losses.

If Jim (the buyer) wants to call off the sale and return the horse, he might be able to sue the seller for "recission," which is a legal remedy comparable to turning back the clock—to go back to the position the buyer and seller would have had if the transaction never took place. In a rescission claim, Jim would demand, *at a minimum*, that the seller take back the horse, refund the full purchase price, and reimburse Jim for all of his expenses in keeping the horse (such as boarding fees, hauling fees, pre-purchase examination fees, routine veterinary expenses, farrier expenses, and others).

Rescission cases can be complex. Courts are hesitant to intervene, unless there is strong proof that the circumstances and law warrant a reversal of the action that has already taken place. Cases involving rescission sometimes require proof that the sales transaction resulted from a fraudulent deception. That is, the buyer would claim that the seller promised that the seller had transferable breed registration papers, when, in reality, the seller had none.

3. Sue the seller for the difference between the horse's value with papers (which the buyer *thought* he or she had bought) and the horse's value without the papers (which the buyer now has).

This option makes sense for those who still want to keep the horse, even without papers, but who want to be reimbursed for the overpayment. In a lawsuit of this type, the buyer would prove that there is a difference between the horse's value *with* breed registration papers and *without* them, and the buyer would ask the seller to pay back the difference. Expert testimony of an equine appraiser might be necessary to prove the different values.

4. Sue the seller for a violation of an applicable state's consumer protection law, deceptive trade practice law, or for violations of a state's Uniform Commercial Code, if applicable.

Complexities in the law, and the differences among the states, make it important to discuss these options with a lawyer.

Can the Breed Registry
Change the Owner on the Papers?

What if the horse buyer simply called or wrote to the horse's breed registry, explained the situation, and asked it to transfer the horse's registration papers into the buyer's name? Would the registry comply? Unlikely.

Each year, breed registries receive numerous requests to transfer registration papers into someone's name without written approval of the last registered owner. These requests arise in a variety of settings, including, for example:

- If a horse is owned by a two-person partnership, one of the partners might claim that the partnership has ended and ask the registry to change the horse's ownership into his or her name only, leaving out the "former" partner's name from the papers.

- While a divorce case proceeds in the legal system, one spouse might ask the breed registry to transfer the horse's registration papers into his or her name only, leaving out the name of the other spouse.

- Someone may buy a horse from a boarding stable that claimed to be holding a "stablemen's lien sale" of the horse (as the stable's way of collecting unpaid boarding fees), but the stable may not have followed the requirements for these sales that are established under the law. Without written approval from the last owner, and without proof that the lien sale complied with the law, the new owner might ask the registry to transfer someone else's papers into her name.

Breed registries, because they risk being sued if they make a hasty judgment, proceed cautiously before transferring papers without a written authorization from the horse's owner of record. In the example above, the breed registry runs too great a risk of making a mistake because it has no signed transfer of ownership form from the horse's last recorded owner. The buyer has nothing in writing to prove that he or she is the horse's valid buyer.

When these requests come in, registries usually take no action. For the protection of themselves and their members, they often wait until the legal issues have been fully resolved in a court of law and after the court has issued a legally binding ruling. In other situations, the registry might only want the buyer or seller to produce an attorney's opinion letter that carefully explains how the applicable state's law entitles the transfer of registration papers without written approval from the last recorded horse owner.

Do Registration Papers Really Prove Ownership?

Not necessarily. In fact, a few courts that have addressed this issue have recognized that the last recorded owner on the horses's registration papers may not be the horse's true owner.

How Do You Avoid Registration Paper Disputes?

Insist on a written sales contract. Written contracts might not prevent every sales dispute, but they can narrow disputes a great deal. A simple sales contract can take as little as five minutes to write. [*Equine Law & Horse Sense* explains how to draft "the five minute sales contract."]

In particular, two essential ingredients of a sales contract which could have prevented the scenario with Jim the buyer are (1) the seller's warranty (promise) that he owns the horse and is legally capable of transferring ownership to the buyer, and (2) a requirement that the seller will immediately transfer breed registration papers into the buyer's name, in a form required by the breed registries.

Ask to see the horse's current breed registration papers. Maybe the seller does not have any registration papers. Or, maybe the horse has never been registered *anywhere*, but the seller has lied about this. Before parting with your money, demand to see the registration papers now.

Consider contacting the breed registry before buying the horse. Some breed registries might help you identify the horse's last recorded owner of record. For example, the American Quarter Horse Association and American Paint Horse Association Records Department will provide this information—even over the telephone and free of charge. This may help confirm the seller's interest in the horse. Keep in mind, however, that there might be other (non-recorded) owners of the horse.

Selling a Horse on Installment Payments? Know the Pitfalls Before You Leap

Banks do it. Credit card issuers do it. Horses can be expensive, and buyers often ask sellers to spread out their payments over months, or even years. Should you, the horse seller, do it?

Whether you are a lending institution or a horse seller, the business of extending credit can be very risky. Horse sellers, banks, and credit card companies have much in common when they agree to extend financing to someone. All of them are undertaking a risk that the buyers will make payments faithfully and honor all of their obligations.

But that is where the similarities end. Banks and credit card companies recognize that extending credit brings tremendous risks. Because of this, they protect themselves well, relying on credit checks, financial disclosures, and detailed contracts before they ever agree to extend credit.

Despite the many risks that come with extending credit, horse sellers often part with a valuable horse merely on a handshake and with only a tiny fraction of the purchase price paid up front—just minutes after meeting a total stranger who wants to buy their horse.

As a result, installment payment disputes occur frequently in the horse industry. Many of these disputes can be avoided when those who *act* like a bank are more willing to *think* and *act* like one, too.

The four most common problems with installment payment arrangements are:

- The buyer stops making payment
- The horse becomes injured, ill, or dies before the buyer makes the final payment
- The seller has to repossess the horse
- The seller is either paid in full or has repossessed the horse—but it took a fortune in legal fees to get this result

Problems in Installment Payment Arrangements and Ways to Address Them

In an installment payment arrangement, the horse seller and buyer agree that the buyer can pay off the purchase price through a series of payments (often called installments) that are spread out over months, and sometimes even years. All installment payment arrangements concerning horses are not alike.

For example, some sellers will readily transfer a horse's breed registration papers into the buyer's name before the horse is fully paid for. Some sellers demand most of the purchase price to be paid up front. Some sellers insist on keeping possession of the horse until all or most of the payments have been made. Other sellers are much more casual about the arrangements, transferring papers, requiring little money down, and allowing the horse to go to the buyer before he is paid for. But the more casual the arrangement, the greater risk the seller takes.

Here are the four most common risks, and ways to minimize them:

1. The Buyer Stops Making Payment

The most common risk in an installment payment arrangement is also the most foreseeable—the buyer might not finish paying for the horse. How can you, as the seller, avoid this? For starters, here are two simple ideas:

Hold the registration papers until the final payment clears the bank. Especially if the horse's value for racing, showing, or breeding purposes depends on the registration papers, you would be wise to retain the papers in your own name and to hold them until the buyer's final installment payment has cleared the bank. This alone is strong motivation for some buyers to pay on time, and sometimes to even make early payments.

Properly document your right to repossess. A carefully written installment sales contract can give you a security interest in the horse, include a legally proper UCC (Uniform Commercial Code) financing statement in a form required under the applicable state's law, and specify from the beginning how and when you may repossess the horse. Without proper documentation, repossession is not easy. Over the years, horse sellers have entered another's property, such as a private barn or pasture, in an attempt to repossess a horse, only to face costly legal battles and sometimes even *criminal charges* of trespass and theft, as a result.

2. The Horse Becomes Injured, Ill, or Dies Before the Buyer Makes the Final Payment

What if the horse, while left in the buyer's care, becomes lame or sick? Even worse, what if the horse dies before you the seller have been fully paid? When these unfortunate events occur, some buyers simply stop making payments. Of the many ways to avoid this problem, here are two:

Carefully address the issue of "risk of loss" in the sales contract. For the seller's protection, an installment sales contract can specify that the buyer shall exclusively bear all risk of the horse's loss after the horse has been delivered to the buyer or after the buyer has signed the contract. This means that the *buyer* will accept the risk of injury to or loss of the horse, and that the buyer is still responsible for paying the full sale price, as agreed.

To address risk of loss, the contract could state, for example:

> All risks of loss and diminution of value of the horse, for whatever cause or reason whatsoever, shall pass to the Buyer as of this date: _____ .

Obviously, this language can be modified (or omitted) to suit the interests of the buyer or seller.

Insure the horse. Insurance cannot prevent a horse's illness or death, but it can protect both parties if something should happen to the horse before the final payment is made. The sales contract can require the buyer to purchase a policy of full mortality insurance on the horse, which designates the seller to receive certain proceeds in the event that a claim is made (this is often called naming you, the seller, as a "loss payee" on the insurance policy). For the buyer's protection, and to prevent the seller from reaping a windfall from collecting installments and also an insurance payout, the contract can specify that you, in the event that insurance proceeds are paid out, can only accept insurance proceeds equal to the amount of the remaining installments, and the rest will go to the buyer.

3. The Seller is Either Paid in Full or Has Repossessed the Horse—But It Took a Fortune in Legal Fees To Get This Result

Installment sales arrangements can, and do, generate costly legal battles. Banks are always prepared for the prospect of legal action and often keep a staff of lawyers for this purpose. But ordinary people selling a horse often have limited funds to hire a lawyer, and most horse owners and facilities do not have lawyers on staff or on retainer. Here are two options for addressing the problem:

Address attorney's fees in the sales contract. For the seller's protection, a sales contract can specify that the buyer agrees to pay the seller's legal fees if a legal dispute should arise involving the contract.

63

Or, the contract can state that the losing party must pay the winning party's legal fees. Unfortunately, there is never a guarantee that a court will enforce attorney fee provisions. Without them, however, you (the seller) have very little chance of recouping the cost of your legal bills.

Include an interest rate clause in the contract. Banks and credit card companies charge interest on unpaid balances. They do this through carefully written contracts that specify the rate of interest. Their contracts are careful to charge interest within limitations dictated by law.

In equine installment sales contracts, you the seller would be wise to include a legally permissible rate of interest that will be assessed, at a minimum, if the buyer falls behind on payments. Alternatively, and to be cautious, the contract can spell out a rate of interest and state that if the buyer falls behind on payments, the seller can assess that rate "or the highest interest rate allowed by law."

Keep in mind that maximum interest rates that individuals and businesses can charge vary from state to state. Financial institutions usually can charge higher rates of interest, mainly because of the heavy degree of regulation these institutions receive from the government.

Drafting Tips for Installment Payment Contracts

An installment sale contract that is designed to protect the horse seller may include, *at a minimum*, these elements:

- The seller's security interest in the horse
- A signed legally proper UCC (Uniform Commercial Code) financing statement, also known as a UCC-1 form, as required under state law
- When payments must be made, to whom, and for how much
- How and when the seller may repossess the horse
- Who bears the risk of the horse's loss after the horse has been delivered to the buyer or after the buyer has signed the installment sale contract
- Who pays attorney fees if a dispute arises (see Chapters One and Two of this book for language ideas)
- Agreement to submit any disputes to arbitration or mediation, if desired
- Interest rate on unpaid balances, and when interest will be assessed
- When the seller will transfer the registration papers

Good advance planning and carefully written contracts can make an installment sale transaction run smoothly for everyone involved.

LEGAL ASPECTS OF THE TRIAL PERIOD FIVE FORESEEABLE PROBLEMS AND HOW YOU CAN AVOID THEM

"Try out my horse for few weeks. See if you get along with him." These were the words of a sincere, well-intentioned seller who only wanted a good home for his horse and a satisfied buyer. The seller expected the buyer, after two weeks, to fall in love with the horse and then pay a fair sale price. Could anything possibly go wrong with this trial period arrangement?

Absolutely it can! Trial periods are popular in equine sales, but unless they are well-defined, you are asking for trouble. In a typical trial period arrangement, a trainer may take a horse "on consignment" from the owner with the goal of attracting a buyer and then sending payment to the seller. Or, a cautious buyer might want to try out a horse for a while before deciding whether to make a purchase.

Where horses are involved, trial period arrangements often involve:

- The buyer paying the seller little or no money until later, *if* the deal goes through

- The buyer hauling away the horse to an unspecified place for "testing"

- No written contract

When done in this manner, trial period arrangements invite problems. This section addresses 5 of the possible problems with trial period arrangements and ways you can avoid them.

Summary of the Most Common Problems in Trial Period Arrangements

The most foreseeable problems with trial periods are:

- The "buyer" steals the horse

- The "buyer" gets hurt during the trial period

- Someone else gets hurt during the trial period and seeks money from the horse's owner

- The "buyer" returns the horse in lame or sick condition

- The "buyer" keeps the horse at a stable during the trial period but falls behind on payments. Because of the non-payment, the stable prevents the horse's release back to the seller

Ways to Avoid The Most Common Problems

Avoiding a trial period sale dispute, at the most basic level, takes good, plain common sense. However, people who have run into problems with these arrangements generally wish that they had used common sense and had taken effective precautions. Let's look at these problems and preventatives in more detail.

1. The "buyer" steals the horse

Among every seller's biggest fears is a "buyer" who asks for a trial period, promises payment later, and then hauls away the horse, never to be seen again. While this situation is not common, when it happens it is a major disruption to peoples' lives. Here are three ways to prevent it:

Require full payment up front. Complete the sale now, but you (the seller) give the buyer the option of returning the horse for a full refund, assuming that the horse is returned in a certain number of days and in good condition. This arrangement has all the advantages of a trial period without the risk of non-payment.

Keep the registration papers until the last payment clears. Papers may mean nothing to the "buyer" whose real intention is to steal the horse and head straight for the nearest auction. But the buyer who needs the horse's papers for breeding, racing, or showing will more likely come through if the seller keeps the papers during the trial period and signs them over after the buyer makes full payment.

Document the transaction as a lease, with the "buyer's" option to buy. Change the transaction to a lease with an option to buy. You can ask the "buyer" to sign a lease agreement (Chapter Four discusses leases and elements of these agreements), that includes an option to change the transaction into a sale under terms you find acceptable. While the lease goes on, you the seller will keep the registration papers until the "buyer" has paid off the horse.

2. The "buyer" gets injured (or worse) during the trial period while riding or handling the horse

Another major concern, as seller, is the prospect for liability during the trial period. After all, in most trial period arrangements, you (the seller) retain ownership of the horse, and there is no telling what the buyer will do to "test out" the horse or how good a rider the buyer may be. With this in mind, the seller can protect himself or herself by doing a few things:

Make the "buyer" sign a well-written release of liability (where allowed by law). As the seller, you are wise to insist that the buyer sign a well-written release of liability, in addition to the trial period contract. Where allowed by law, a release of liability (sometimes called a "waiver") is a powerful protection for those who own horses. A release is someone's agreement to sign away what could otherwise be a legal right to sue for possibly millions of dollars. What goes into a well-written release of liability can vary in each state. If you want the best protection, consult with a knowledgeable attorney.

Insurance. Although courts in most states have enforced properly worded and presented liability releases, having good insurance remains a must. As a cautious seller, make sure that your insurance is up to date as to types and amounts of coverage and that the insurance will cover injuries that might happen during the trial period. Horse owners might want to buy a policy of Personal Horse Owner's Liability Insurance. Discuss this with your insurance agent.

Make the transaction a sale that can be reversed. You the seller can request that the horse be sold, with the buyer entitled to a refund under certain conditions—preferably in writing. This arrangement will not end your liability, however. The fact is, you can always be sued for breach of contract, fraud, or other legal theories, especially if there is evidence that you knew, but wrongfully hid from the buyer, the very dangerous propensities that caused an injury.

3. Someone else gets injured (or worse) during the trial period

Simply because you own the horse, you are at risk of being named a party in a lawsuit if the horse kicks, bites, throws, or injures someone during the trial period or even if the person becomes injured due to no fault of the horse (this could happen, for example, if the person falls off or lacks the skills to ride at the canter). Certainly, many of the same suggestions found in Problem 2, above, apply to this scenario.

In addition, sellers should be aware of *indemnification*. The word is big, but in its most basic sense, indemnification is an arrangement in which someone agrees to pay another for a loss or liability that may occur. For instance, an indemnification agreement in a trial period contract can state that if anyone should bring a suit or claim against the seller, when the seller was not at fault for the injury or loss, then the buyer agrees to pay the seller's legal fees and any losses or liabilities or judgments that anyone might claim against the seller.

4. The "buyer" returns the horse in lame or sick condition

You (the seller) can seek to protect yourself from the situation in which the buyer calls off the sale and returns the horse in lame or sick condition. For example:

Keep the horse on your property during the trial period. If the horse stays on the property belonging to you (the seller) or at the boarding stable where the seller keeps the horse, during the trial period, you can better make sure it is well-tended and not being abused. You can also guard against the horse being put in unsafe situations, such as tied to a tractor. Also, you can set basic rules for the horse's use during the trial period, such as hours for use, places where the horse can be ridden, and what the buyer can and cannot do. You will also be there to see that the horse gets prompt veterinary care, if needed.

Buy insurance. Before the trial period starts, talk with your insurance agent. Your mortality or major medical insurance could be at issue if the horse's health takes a turn for the worse while kept somewhere else during a trial period. The problem is, the buyer might not know of the need to contact the insurer right away when something goes wrong. Or, the trial period arrangement might void your insurance coverage.

5. The "buyer" boards the horse at a stable during the trial period but falls behind on payments. Because of non-payment, the stable prevents the horse's release back to the seller

Stablemen's lien laws can complicate trial periods. That is, the laws of most states give boarding stables a lien on horses. Many of these laws also state that, when the stable has not been paid, it may keep possession of the horses and even sell them (with legal restrictions that differ in each state). Because of these laws, you (the seller) risk losing the horse and not receiving advance notice that the stable is holding a stablemen's lien sale.

What can you the seller do? Of the many options available, here are two:

Approve the boarding stable in advance. If you agree to part with your horse during the trial period, make sure you know *and approve* the boarding stable where the horse will be kept. You can see that the stable knows, *at a minimum*, your name, address, and the fact that you own the horse. You can ask to be contacted if there is any difficulty with the boarder or his payment (such as a bounced check).

Require that the buyer fully pre-pay board to cover the trial period. You the seller can demand that the buyer fully pre-pay all board and fees that may become due during the trial period. This reduces the risk that the boarding stable will seek drastic remedies to get paid.

HOLD EVERYTHING!
INJUNCTION PROCEEDINGS IN THE HORSE INDUSTRY

Brian (the buyer) thought the stallion was his. A few days ago, he gave Steve (the seller) a sizeable good faith deposit on the purchase of a stallion, with the understanding that the purchase arrangements would be finalized later in the week. However, the day Brian brought his final payment, Steve refused it, handed back the deposit, and told Brian that the deal was off because he was selling the stallion to somebody else across the country. Brian insists on buying the stallion, and he wants to enforce his agreement before the horse leaves the state. What can he do?

In the example above, Brian (the buyer) may have legal grounds to seek an *injunction* against Steve the seller through the court system.

Few people in the horse industry have ever heard of injunctions. This little-known but powerful proceeding has a place in many equine disputes, especially sales transactions. This section explores injunctions, what they are, how lawyers pursue them, and alternatives.

What is an Injunction?

An injunction is a legal ruling issued by a judge that either requires a party to undertake some specified act or prohibits a party from carrying out a specific act. The ruling is enforceable and powerful enough to stop an event or action from taking place. For example, if Brian were serious about buying Steve's stallion, Brian's lawyer could consider promptly seeking an injunction that, at a minimum, would force Steve to halt any sale of the stallion to *anyone* until the court rules on whether Brian's right to buy the stallion (if he, in fact, has one) takes priority over the would-be buyer from another state.

Over the years, the more publicized injunctions are those that force striking workers back to their jobs, and halt demolition crews who are about to demolish historic buildings. In the horse industry, injunction proceedings can be appropriate in these settings and many others:

- Sales disputes, such as in the example with Brian, above
- Legal action to stop a horse show from denying a horse entry into a specified class

- Legal action to stop a horse trainer from working at a nearby stable because the trainer has violated a lawful agreement not to compete with a former employer

How Can You Obtain an Injunction?

In the eyes of the law, an injunction is considered an extraordinary legal remedy, mainly because it has the effect of changing the way things are. These proceedings are best handled through a lawyer, not on your own, because of the intensive review courts give these matters. Usually, courts will only evaluate injunction requests if they are made in writing and in a very formal way. The judge will be looking for carefully researched briefs and plenty of detail.

Careful planning also goes into the selection of a court. For example, if the injunction involves a horse, the court located in the county where the horse lives typically has legal authority to issue an injunction that affects the horse's whereabouts.

Three Basic Types of Injunctions

Generally, there are three types of injunctions:

1. Temporary Restraining Order

Where allowed by law, the buyer would start with this. Brian's lawyer would quickly ask the court—without Steve the seller knowing it—to issue a Temporary Restraining Order. This document, by its terms, stops Steve (the seller) from moving or selling the stallion until the court can more fully evaluate the matter in a few days. At that later date, the court will hold a preliminary or temporary injunction hearing.

The function of a Temporary Restraining Order is to keep things as they are for a short period of time until the judge can hear both sides of the story and examine the applicable law. Only the judge has the power to make these rulings—a demand letter written by you or your lawyer cannot do this.

2. Preliminary Injunction or Temporary Injunction

Within only a few days after the court issues a Temporary Restraining Order, the court typically holds a special hearing. In Brian's case, the court would use this hearing to decide whether a preliminary injunction (sometimes called a temporary injunction) should be issued to stop the horse's sale to someone else and, if so, under what terms. This preliminary injunction is a more long-lasting legal command than the Temporary Restraining Order.

By the time the hearing takes place, Steve will now be aware of the legal proceedings. He will want his lawyer to be present. The court, at the preliminary injunction hearing, will consider several factors, including:

- The court will evaluate whether the one who seeks the preliminary injunction (Brian, the buyer) has a strong chance of winning, should the case against Steve continue through the legal system. That is, Brian would likely prove that the law gives him the legal right to buy the stallion, with priority over everyone else. Steve might argue that Brian had no legitimate contract and that Brian should lose his case.

- The court will also evaluate whether Brian would suffer "irreparable injury" if no injunction were issued. Here, for example, Steve might contend that Brian would suffer no harm if he lost the stallion because there are plenty of good stallions available for purchase, and any "harm" Brian suffers can be compensated by money, anyway. Brian might argue that this particular stallion is so unique that the most appropriate remedy is an injunction, which would award him the right to buy *that* particular stallion.

- The court will consider whether granting an injunction serves the public interest. Brian would likely argue that the public interest favors enforcing valid contracts.

After the judge explores these (and possibly other) factors at the hearing, he or she will decide whether a preliminary injunction should be issued and, if so, under what terms.

3. Permanent Injunction

After all of these steps, the next question is whether to make the injunction permanent. After a full hearing or trial on the merits takes place, the court can issue (or not issue) a permanent injunction. By this time, lawyers for Brian and Steve will make sure that the court has considered all issues.

What Happens if Someone Refuses to Comply With an Injunction?

If Steve refused to comply with a properly issued injunction or restraining order, the court can penalize him with a jail sentence, fine, or other monetary penalty.

Alternatives to the Injunction

Because injunction proceedings can be expensive, they are not right for every matter or budget. Some alternatives exist. For example, if Brian the buyer decided not to pursue an injunction, or even if he lost his injunction efforts, he still might have a lawsuit against Steve the seller due to Steve's failure to complete the sale. Here, however, Brian's lawsuit would ask Steve to pay him money—not give him the stallion.

Conclusion

In conclusion, please keep these ideas in mind:

1. With injunctions, timing can be critical. This means that, in a situation like this, Brian the buyer should explore this legal option *quickly* after learning that the seller was about to sell the horse to someone else. Timing is especially important because injunctions are usually issued by the court located in the county where the horse is maintained. In the example above, Steve planned to sell the stallion to someone outside the state. If Brian waited too long, he would risk losing track of the stallion. Filing his injunction case in the wrong court will lose valuable time, as well, since the wrong court has no power to act.

2. State laws often tell which courts have the power to handle injunctions. Because injunctions are considered special types of relief, certain courts—such as small claims courts—may be powerless to issue them.

3. Injunctions are not easy, nor are they cheap. These proceedings can be highly complex and often require extensive legal analysis, which lawyers must give the court through written briefs, hearings, affidavits, and witness testimony.

4. Aside from the legal cost, injunctions might have other costs, as well, such as a bond. For example, let's say that the court issues a preliminary injunction that gives Brian the buyer temporarily possession of the stallion—before the court has resolved all of the legal issues for good. Knowing that this decision might be reversed down the line, the court might also order Brian to deposit a *cash bond* with the court. The cash bond would likely equal some or all of the stallion's value. By paying the bond (sometimes depositing the money directly with the court, if the court so requests), Brian is promising that he is a willing and able buyer who can meet his obligations.

How Legal Are Your Advertisements?

Most people and business involved with horses, sooner or later, advertise in horse related magazines, newspapers, and web-sites. But few equine professionals know much about advertising and the legal pitfalls that might place them in violation of a state or federal law. If you are the one having a dispute with an advertiser, it helps to know your legal rights.

This section generally discusses the laws associated with advertising, as well as defenses and how to avoid a dispute from your advertisements.

What is Deceptive Advertising?

Just because an advertisement is inaccurate does not always make it illegal. You may disagree with the quality of an advertisement but this might not measure up to a valid lawsuit, either. The law expects advertisements to be accurate about important aspects of the item or the service that is offered for sale. Also, a deceptive advertisement must deceive the buyer in an important way (or, as the law calls it, in a "material way"). For example:

- An expensive bridle that looks nicer in the catalog than on your horse may not support a lawsuit, unless, of course, the bridle you bought lacks important features of the one advertised, such as brass buckles.

- If a stallion's advertised photograph puts him in a nice pose, such as with a beautifully outstretched neck, but the stallion looks a bit different in person, this may not give you a case, either. However, if the photograph was retouched to lengthen and trim the stallion's neck, or if the photograph was retouched to change the stallion's conformation, that would be deceptive.

- If you are a mare owner seeking to produce a sizeable foal from your small mare, you might have a lawsuit against the stallion owner who sold you a breeding to a stallion advertised as being 16.2 hands tall, when the horse was only 15.2 hands. Your case would be weakened if you cared only about the stallion's markings, athleticism, and lineage, and not his height. In that setting, the advertisement did not "materially mislead" you.

State and Federal Laws That Regulate and Prohibit Deceptive Advertisements

State laws. False and deceptive advertisements violate several laws on a state and federal level. At least 33 states across the country have laws that prohibit deceptive advertising; those states include (but may not be limited to) Alaska, Arizona, Arkansas, California, Colorado, Delaware, Georgia, Hawaii, Idaho, Illinois, Indiana, Iowa, Kansas, Kentucky, Louisiana, Maryland, Michigan, Minnesota, Mississippi, Missouri, Nevada, New Jersey, New Mexico, North Carolina, North Dakota, Ohio, Oklahoma, South Dakota, Tennessee, Texas, Utah, West Virginia, and Wyoming.

One common—and unlawful—deceptive advertising practice is the "bait and switch" scheme. When this happens, an advertiser purposely under-prices an item or service, with no intention of selling at the advertised price. The advertiser's goal is to "bait" people to respond, so that the advertiser can "switch" the buyer's interest to buy a slightly different, but much more costly, item or service.

States often have Deceptive Trade Practices Acts and/or Consumer Protection Acts on the books. Among other things, these laws prohibit deceptive practices in trade or commerce. Deceptive and misleading advertisements risk violating these laws.

Federal laws. The Federal Trade Commission (FTC) Act regulates advertising and deceptive trade practices. It prohibits "unfair methods of competition in commerce and unfair or deceptive acts or practices in commerce" and makes unlawful advertisements that are "misleading in a material respect." In addition, the FTC requires a "reasonable basis" for the claims made in advertisements.

Another federal law involving advertisements is the Lanham Act. This law applies to advertisements that were made "in commerce" and makes advertisers legally answerable for certain misrepresentations in their advertisements. A person or business can sue the advertiser in a state or federal court for violation of this law.

Action Against Unlawful Advertisers

Deceptive advertising doesn't pay. Just one deceptive advertisement could place the advertiser at risk of being sued by many people, businesses, and even the government—all at the same time. For example:

- The Federal Trade Commission (FTC) in Washington, D.C., might take action against a deceptive advertiser. Contact the FTC at (202) 326-2222. For example, the FTC once found an advertising campaign for a popular mouthwash to be misleading; it required

74

the advertiser to correct its advertisements by running new ads stating: "Contrary to prior advertising, this mouthwash will not help prevent colds or sore throats or lessen their severity."

• The Attorney General's office within a state might take action to stop improper advertisements. In Texas, for example, the Attorney General halted advertisements by a major automaker because of concern that its ads contained misleading information about its cars' safety. Contact your Attorney General's Office, consumer affairs division.

• Unhappy buyers can sue advertisers directly for violation of many of the state and federal laws outlined above. An unhappy buyer might also have recourse against a seller if an item does not fit the statements in an advertisement. Sellers are especially vulnerable when they advertise, for example, that a horse is "100 per cent sound" or "has no vices or bad habits." If these statements prove untrue at the time of sale, the buyer might bring suit. In this setting, the buyer would claim that the statements in the advertisement were "express warranties" (statements of fact or descriptions of the item on which the buyer relied that could, if untrue, give the buyer legally enforceable rights).

• Competing businesses can sue each other over their ads. Prompted by a competitor's advertisement, for example, a business might sue claiming that the ad defamed (or disparaged) the business in some way. These legal battles usually result from a "comparative advertisement" that compares an advertised item or service to those offered by competitors. Also, businesses can sue one another under theories of unfair competition.

Possible Defenses to Claims of Unlawful Advertising

Advertisers accused of deceptive practices have several available defenses, depending on the circumstances. Here are a few of them:

Truthfulness of the advertisement. The most obvious defense is also the most powerful: the advertisement was completely *truthful*.

No deception took place. Another defense is that the buyer was not deceived, or the advertisement did not materially influence the buyer's decision to buy the advertised item or service.

The statements were mere "puffery" and not misstatements of fact. It is fair and legal to boast—but within limits. Statements of sales talk or boasting (often called "puffery") are common and acceptable for advertising. Puffing has been described as statements of opinion or general or imprecise statements that are not based on reliable facts. As one court explained, "puffery," is in part, "exaggerated advertising, blustering, and boasting upon which no reasonable buyer would rely." Well-known examples of puffing are: "This is a marvelous saddle," "This stallion is the perfect cross on your mares," or "Your next champion will probably come from XYZ Farm."

First Amendment freedom of speech. Despite the power of the First Amendment guarantee of freedom of speech, found in the United States Constitution, this is not guaranteed to shield an advertiser from liability for false or deceptive advertising.

No "bait and switch" took place. A business accused of a "bait and switch" practice may simply have run out of an advertised item. State laws sometimes require merchants to stock a "reasonable" supply of advertised items, with no further obligation on the merchant's part to stock or discount more. Some merchants, however, without a legal obligation to do so, will issue "rain checks" for unavailable advertised items so that the consumer can later buy the product at the discounted price.

No malice. In many cases, advertisers accused of disparaging their business competitors will only be found liable if they acted with "malice" when they placed the complained-of advertisement. Lawsuits claiming disparagement of someone else's service or product can be difficult to win because of the problem of successfully proving "malice."

Cutting the Risks

You can reduce your risk of being sued or running afoul of advertising regulations. Here are some suggestions:

- Before running an ad, carefully check all claims for accuracy, especially if the advertisement contains statements of fact that can be proven. You can show it to others and get their opinions, too.

- Be especially careful when making a "comparative ad" in which you compare your own product, horse, or service to someone else's. Chances are good that the competitor will carefully scrutinize your advertisement for inaccuracies.

- If the statements in your advertisements change over time—such as a stallion's "100 per cent conception rate" or a "new" product or service—you (the advertiser) can change the ad. You can also tell any customers who were attracted to the ad (*before* they part with their money) about the new facts.

- If your advertisement contained a mis-printed price, you can correct the mistake in a later advertisement. Some publications, if they caused the error, will correct the mistake and re-run the ad for free.

CHAPTER FOUR

RELATIONSHIPS WITH OTHERS INVOLVING HORSES — BOARDING, TRAINING, SHARING, AND LEASING HORSES

The Horse Owner's Guide to Achieving a Good Relationship With the Boarding Stable

In most areas, the boarding stable business is no longer a "buyer's market." There are fewer stables, thanks, in large part, to urban sprawl which has turned barns and bridle paths into shopping centers and subdivisions. Boarding stables have also become more businesslike and usually set rules and requirements for their customers. For example, stables often require customers to sign detailed boarding contracts with liability releases.

As a horse owner, what, if any, measures can you take to protect your interests in the horse boarding relationship? This section explores factors that the person who wants to board his horse should think through before doing business with a boarding stable, including:

- What to consider before signing the boarding contract
- What to consider before signing a liability release
- Insurance available to protect the horse owner
- How to negotiate changes to the contract
- How to encourage positive communication with the stable

What to Consider Before Signing the Boarding Contract

As a customer, you are entrusting the stable with your prized possession—your horse. Chances are good that a stretch of days, possibly even a week, may occasionally pass when you cannot visit the stable. This means that you have to rely on the stable to give your horse good-quality of care in your absence.

Before becoming a customer, here are some factors worth evaluating:

The stable management's overall integrity and dedication. Since you will be relying on the integrity, good judgment, and basic common sense of the stable managers, ask good questions before you bring your horse to them. Find out the stable's experience in caring for horses. Ask how the stable would handle foreseeable problems, like a sudden case of colic, your horse getting cast in a stall, or your horse experiencing a serious injury in the pasture. Talk with other boarders about the stable, and ask the stable for references.

Professionalism. The overwhelming majority of stables care about their reputation and their boarders' level of satisfaction. They want to remain an important part of the horse industry. For many stables, this means working long hours to keep the facility clean and well-tended. Some stables go the distance in an effort to please their customers. A small number of stables even provide a "welcome" package of materials for new boarders. Some publish newsletters or hold boarders' meetings when issues of mutual concern arise.

Knowledge and experience. Knowledgeable staff is a vitally important factor in the selection of a boarding stable. However, boarding stable customers who insist on the *most* experienced managers could be missing out on ground-floor opportunities at a fine facilities. For example, many excellent boarding stables are owned by people who, like their customers, were horse boarders at other facilities. When those people launched their own horse boarding businesses, what they lacked in hands-on experience they made up for in their knowledge of horses and dedication to do things better.

With this in mind, and especially if you are evaluating a newly-established boarding stable owned or managed by persons with no previous track record, make sure you are satisfied with the stable management's overall knowledge of horses.

Pride. How healthy do the horses appear? How neat are the tack rooms, stalls, rest rooms, customer areas, and aisles? Are you satisfied with the quality of the hay and feed? Your inspection of a boarding facility and the horses within it will speak volumes about the stable's dedication and pride.

Can you add your assumptions into the contract? In the contract, you (the horse owner) can ask the stable to agree to care for your horse in a particular way. For example, the boarding contract can specify that the stable will give your horse a standard or quality of care commonly associated with facilities that keep good quality show horses, race horses, breeding horses, or (as the case may be) pleasure horses. Or, you might write in specifics (that risk being debated at a later point), such as whether blanketing and un-blanketing or holding a horse for the farrier are included in the board fee.

Health requirements for the horses. Horse owners would be wise to make sure that the stable sets health requirements for horses coming into the stable and living there. Some stables require recent health certificates before a new horse can enter the facility; other stables simply ask the horse owner to represent in writing that the horse has been de-wormed recently and is current on immunizations. A negative Coggin's test should be an absolute minimum.

Safety. Some stables post "stable rules" that are designed to promote the safety and well-being of their horses and boarders. Also, a stable's fences and gates can tell a great deal about its attention to safety. Good fencing minimizes the risk of a horse getting injured in the pasture or escaping onto nearby roads. (Certainly, open range districts, found in a few areas of the country, are the obvious exception because fences are not always required in those areas.)

What to Consider Before Signing a Release of Liability

More than ever, stables and professionals are asking their customers to sign releases of liability (also called "waivers"). These facilities are doing this to protect themselves from legal liability for injuries or losses that may result from their negligence or violations of certain equine liability laws. (Negligence is the failure to act as a reasonably prudent person would act under the circumstances.)

Because waivers and releases can be very powerful under the law in most states, what you sign today, when all seems well, might destroy your legal recourse against the stable if things go bad tomorrow. Before you sign a release or waiver of liability, consider these things:

- Make sure that you understand the document before you sign it
- Make sure that you are satisfied with the stable's reputation
- If you do not agree with the release, chances are good that the stable will not relieve you from signing it; you may have to take your business, and your horse, elsewhere

Protect Your Investment by Insuring Your Horse

Even with the best care, horses can become injured, ill, or die. As protection in case the worst should ever happen, you can purchase your own policy of mortality insurance as well as major medical and surgical insurance, and loss of use insurance. [See *Equine Law & Horse Sense* for detailed information on insurance and negligence.]

Protect Yourself With Your Own Liability Insurance

Your horse—wherever you may stable him—has the potential to hurt somebody. Your horse might bite, kick, or throw someone, whether by accident or on purpose. When someone gets hurt, he or she is likely to sue everybody having any connection to the horse. This means that *both* the horse owner and the boarding stable could be sued. Unfortunately for you, the horse owner, the stable's policy of liability insurance may not defend or protect you.

For your own protection, you can buy insurance that is designed to protect you if someone tries to hold you legally responsible for the actions of your horse. This policy is known as a "Personal Horse Owner's Liability Policy (some insurers call it a "Private Horse Owner's Liability Policy" or "Individual Horse Owner's Liability Policy")," and many equine insurance companies offer it. Never assume that your basic homeowner's policy gives you this protection.

How to Encourage Communication
With the Boarding Stable

Arrange constructive boarder/management meetings. Consider asking for meetings between the stable management and the boarders to discuss important issues of mutual concern. Keep the meetings focused and constructive. If your meetings turn into griping sessions or shouting matches, with personal attacks, you will accomplish nothing and the meetings will never happen again. On the other hand, you can use the meetings to praise good workmanship, recognize someone's good service, cheer for a fellow boarder's competition success and also discuss making an awkward situation, such as crowding at the wash rack, better.

"Buddy up" with a fellow boarder. Chances are good that while you are away from the stable, another boarder is at the barn enjoying his or her horse—and vice versa. A "buddy" system with a fellow boarder (or two) can allow each buddy to check on the care their horses receive when the other buddy is absent. For example, each buddy can agree to check on whether the other buddy's horse is getting feed supplements, enough clean water, and a clean stall. Then, the buddy can notify the other of any problems. This arrangement will encourage communication with the boarding stable, as well.

Limit gossip. If you have a problem, bring it to the stable management or the person who can do something about it. Don't make it a source of gossip among the boarders. This tends to develop an "us-versus-them" mentality, and makes effective communication difficult. It also means that your problem is not getting solved while you are busy talking with the wrong people.

LIABILITY OF THE BOARDING STABLE
FOR INJURIES TO ITS CUSTOMER'S HORSES

Could the following scenario happen to you?

Bill boards a mare at a stable. One morning the stable called Bill with bad news. The previous night, a new employee at the stable accidentally placed the mare in a stall next to a stallion. The stallion had a history, unknown to the new employee, of being fierce when stabled next to mares. The stallion broke down the wall and attacked, nearly killing the mare. Bill's veterinarian advised him that the mare would recover, but the injuries will permanently end her performance career. Bill learned that the stallion had been kept in the same stall for years. Upon inspection of the stall, Bill discovered that the wall separating this stallion from his mare was extremely thin and poorly patched from other mishaps the stallion caused in the past. Bill now wants to sue the stable.

Does Bill have a case? This section explores boarding stable liabilities, including what makes a case, what defenses the stable can raise, and preventive measures the stable can take.

What the Law Expects of a Boarding Stable's Services

When a stable accepts a horse belonging to another for care and keeping—regardless of whether the stable is a two-horse or a 200-horse operation—the law generally imposes a duty on the stable to use "reasonable care." In the eyes of the law, this means that the facility and its employees must use the degree of care that a prudent and careful stable would exercise in similar circumstances. If Bill pursues a claim against the stable, he would be required to prove that the stable fell short of this standard and should be liable (legally accountable) for the damages that have resulted.

The stable's liability in the above example seems clear. First, the stable knew of the stallion's history of terrorizing mares when placed in similar situations. Second, the stable's employee put Bill's mare in a position of danger by placing her in a stall next to this particular stallion.

What the Boarder Stands
to Collect From The Boarding Stable

What damages could Bill (the boarder) recover if he brings a winning case against the boarding stable?

- If the mare died, he would, at a minimum, try to collect the mare's value immediately before the injury plus any out-of-pocket expenses he may have incurred while attempting to bring her back to health, such as veterinary expenses or hauling fees.

- If the mare lives, Bill would seek the amount of money that the mare decreased in value as a result of the stable's mis-deed, plus reimbursement for the out of pocket expenses that Bill paid in bringing the mare back to health. Depending on the circumstances, he might also seek the value of any lost foals or lost net earnings from races or shows, if the mare's condition keeps her from these activities.

The Stable's Defenses

Here are some defenses the stable might try to assert:

"It was only a mistake and no legal consequences should follow." A "mistake" will not be a valid defense to a claim of negligence. Negligence, by its most basic definition, means the failure to act reasonably. Consequently, people or businesses could be negligent *even* when they have no intention of inflicting harm on someone's person or property.

"The employee did it—not the stable." What if the stable should argue that its newest *employee*, who apparently was unaware of the stallion's dangerous history, should take the blame? That defense will likely fail, as well. Typically, a business is responsible for the negligent acts its employees commit on the job. Also, the law in the applicable state might charge the employee with knowledge that the employer had—such as the knowledge that this particular stallion was a hazard to mares—even if this was not in fact the case.

"The stallion's owner is to blame." The stable might assert that the stallion's owner should take the blame because the stallion, not the stable, inflicted the injuries. Even if the stable could hold the stallion's owner accountable for some of the problem, this assertion will not completely relieve the stable from liability in this situation. Here, the stable maintained the stallion for an extensive period of time, knew of the stallion's dangerousness, and arguably could have prevented the problem. Indeed, the stallion's owner might have a claim of his or her own against the stable for negligent care of the stallion.

Damage Control for the Stable

What measures could the stable have taken to prevent the problem? Here are a few:

Insurance. Insurance may not prevent problems from happening, but it could spare the stable of the burden of hiring a lawyer or settling disputes with the stable's own funds. Many boarding stables are surprised to learn that standard provisions in their commercial general liability insurance policies typically offer no protection for situations like this where a boarder complains that the stable gave his horse negligent care. However, stables that purchase "Care, Custody, and Control" insurance would likely be protected. "Care, custody, and control" insurance (some companies call it "care custody, *or* control" insurance or a "bailee coverage legal liability" policy) is usually issued as a special endorsement to a commercial general liability insurance policy. This type of coverage is designed to protect the stable against claims involving horses that are injured while in the stable's care, custody, and control due to the stable's own negligence.

Careful training of employees. As a general matter, employers are legally responsible for the negligent acts their employees commit on the job. Stables should make every effort to train their workers well.

Boarding contracts, including liability releases. Can boarders, such as Bill, release stables from liability for the consequences of the stable's own negligence in the stabling of a horse? Yes. In many states, this is perfectly legal, if done through proper language in the contracts. Below is an example of how a boarding contract used by a Kentucky stable several years ago addressed a release of liability pertaining to the boarded horse:

> The Stable shall not be liable for any injury or damage to the Horse, including but not limited to, loss by fire, theft, running away, disease, accident, death, or injury, whether the Horse be on the premises of the Stable or not. The Owner shall be solely responsible for all acts and behavior of the Horse at any time and hereby agrees to indemnify and hold the Stable harmless against all damages sustained or suffered by reason of the boarding of the Horse and for any claims or injuries whatsoever arising out of or in any way relating to the Horse.

Does The Stable Look Guilty if It Takes Corrective Action After the Mishap?

In the example at the beginning, the stable might be afraid to overhaul the damaged wall or fire its careless employee after the mare was hurt, out of fear that these measures would be viewed as an admission of negligence or wrongdoing. This view is a mistake.

Under the rules of evidence in most states, the stable is *encouraged* to make the repairs, without fear that they will serve as evidence of negligence against it. In fact, courtroom evidence rules commonly state that these corrective measures after a mishap are not admissible in a court of law to prove negligence. Lawyers might possibly use the evidence for other purposes, however.

LEGAL ASPECTS OF THE "HALF-LEASE"/ SHARE BOARDING ARRANGEMENT

Geri loves her horse, Traveler, and especially enjoys their evening rides together after Geri finishes work. But Geri's schedule is changing. Her employer has just promoted her, and her new position will require longer work hours and more travel. As happy as Geri is to receive the promotion, she knows that this will give her less time to spend with her beloved Traveler.

Mike takes riding lessons at the stable where Geri keeps Traveler. Mike has plenty of time to ride and has approached Geri with an idea. He would like to pay part of Traveler's expenses in exchange for some riding time. This way, the horse will receive more care and attention, even when Geri is not available.

Should Geri enter into this arrangement with Mike? What should she consider before saying yes?

Before the horse-sharing arrangement (sometimes called a "half-lease" or "share board" arrangement) begins, all parties should discuss these five questions:

- Who will pay for the horse's upkeep?
- What if the horse needs major veterinary care?
- What if somebody gets hurt, and what can the parties do to protect themselves against personal injury lawsuits?
- Are there limits on the use of the horse?
- Is a written contract necessary?

This section addresses several of these questions below. It also explains elements to consider for a contract covering this arrangement.

Five Key Issues in a "Half-Lease" or "Share Board" Arrangement

1. Who Pays For the Horse's Upkeep?

When two or more people share the use of a horse, it seems reasonable that they should share the horse's basic expenses and

87

upkeep—expenses such as boarding stable fees, hoof trimming and shoeing and routine veterinary care.

2. What If the Horse Needs Major Veterinary Care?

The possibility always exists that an emergency will arise, bringing a huge veterinary bill (or, in some cases, forcing an immediate decision to end the horse's life). For example, the horse might experience a severe cut during a trail ride, lameness after a strenuous workout, or colic. If either of these things should happen while the horse-sharing arrangement is in effect, who will pay the veterinarian's bill?

As unpleasant as these issues are, they are foreseeable. In a carefully written contract, the parties can address them in advance. As examples:

- Some contracts provide that the one responsible for causing the horse's malady, or the last one to use the horse before the problem occurs, must pay the veterinary expenses. The problem is, because the parties are sharing in the horse's use, there might be no way to determine who or what caused a malady, such as colic.

- In some contracts, the parties agree to split the cost of a policy of mortality and major medical insurance on the horse.

3. What if Somebody Gets Hurt?

People can, and sometimes do, get hurt around horses. This is a risk we all face. But is Geri willing to accept this risk while Mike rides her horse? Geri will fear that Mike will sue her if he is hurt while riding or near Traveler.

Geri has a few options:

Insurance. Geri could purchase a policy of liability insurance designed to protect her if Mike, or anyone else, should bring a claim or a lawsuit against her based on Traveler's actions. One type of insurance commonly available is a Personal Horse Owner's Liability policy (sometimes called a "Private" Horse Owner's Liability policy). Geri can discuss this, and other advisable coverages, with her insurance agent.

Release of liability (where allowed by law). Where allowed by law, Geri could also ask Mike to sign a carefully worded release of liability (sometimes called a "waiver").

Indemnification agreement. In her contract with Mike, Geri could insist on carefully worded indemnification language, in which Mike agrees to protect Geri, hold her harmless, pay her legal expenses, and pay any other costs if someone sues Geri because of injuries or damages that Mike caused.

4. Are There Limits on the Use of the Horse?

Geri might want to set limits on what Mike can do with Traveler. For example, she might want to keep Mike from hauling or showing the horse. She can ask Mike to affirm these limits in a contract.

5. Is a Written Contract Necessary?

The half-lease/share boarding arrangement, like many other arrangements with horses, can work best when the parties put their terms and responsibilities in writing. Below are several elements for these contracts.

Drafting Tips for Half-Lease/ Share Boarding Contracts

A contract for the half-lease/share boarding arrangement can include, *at a minimum*:

- When the arrangement begins and ends
- When each party can use the horse
- Uses of the horse that are permitted and not permitted
- When payments, such as the horse's upkeep expenses, must be made, and to whom (such as the paying the boarding stable, farrier, or others directly)
- Who, if anyone, must pay major expenses, such as veterinary expenses for serious injuries, illnesses, or lameness problems that may arise during the arrangement
- Location of the horse
- Liability waiver/release and indemnification language (where allowed by law)
- Equine Activity Liability Act language (See Chapter 2 of this book)
- How either party can end the arrangement
- Which state's law applies
- How any legal disputes will be addressed and where
- Who, if anyone, pays legal fees if a dispute arises

With careful planning and a good contract, the "half-lease"/share boarding arrangement could keep the parties, and the horse, happy for a long time.

How to Achieve a Positive Relationship With Your Horse Trainer

What do horse trainers and automobile mechanics have in common? Not much. Cars can be fixed, but training is an ongoing process. Mechanics usually can estimate the time and cost needed to restore a car to good performance, but few horse trainers can estimate how much time it will take to turn a horse into a polished performer.

The trainer/customer relationship creates fertile ground for several types of disputes. Here are a few that really happened:

- *A horse becomes seriously ill or lame while in the trainer's care, but the trainer might not notify the owner before deciding to seek (or not seek) veterinary attention.*

- *A horse owner, after visiting the trainer's facility a few times but not seeing his horse actively involved in training, might assume that the trainer has done nothing to earn her money and, on that basis, refuse to pay the training fee.*

- *After years of training and thousands of dollars spent in fees, the owner might receive long-overdue news from the trainer: the horse is simply not capable of being trained for the activities the owner desired.*

The people involved in these disputes seriously considered pursuing legal action. These and other disputes can be avoided, if the parties consider these eight practical suggestions:

- Discuss goals
- Make promises you can reasonably keep
- Communicate, especially when problems arise
- Use written contracts
- Remember how insurance applies
- Focus on professionalism
- If a dispute arises, think before acting out or speaking out
- Try to end the relationship without "bad blood"

Each of these suggestions is discussed below.

90

Discuss Goals

Why wait before discussing training goals? The best time to start is *before* the trainer/client relationship begins. Performance matters are subjective, and it is important to make sure that both you and the trainer are specific about the goals and what it will take to achieve them. Maybe the client wants a hot-off-the-track Thoroughbred to become a competitive Class A-caliber jumper. Maybe the client believes his horse can become a top-notch Western Pleasure winner. Maybe neither of these clients wants to keep the horse in training for more than two months. Experience might tell the trainer from the start that the client's goals are unreasonable or unattainable.

Certainly, trainers may have a vested interest in continuing mutually beneficial training relationships, but they should speak up promptly if they are not the right person to take the horse to that level, if a horse seems incapable of achieving the customer's goals, or if the customer is not skilled enough to achieve his goals with the horse. Communication will give the client the chance to decide which direction to take: sell the horse, "take a gamble" by spending more money on training, pursue different goals, or get another opinion. Communication can also help prevent bitter feelings in the future.

Make Promises You Can Reasonably Keep

Can a trainer legitimately promise: "I will double your money on this horse after only three months of training," or "This will be a National Champion horse this fall, just give me a summer to train him"? The answer depends on the applicable law. Typically, however, the trainer's optimistic statements of "puffing" and hype are usually not a strong basis of a fraud or misrepresentation claim by the horse owner.

Promises of future performance are likely to create unrealistic expectations. Trainers can fairly and safely promise that they will use their *best efforts* to train a horse to satisfy their clients' goals and then, of course, carry out their actions to live up to those promises.

Communicate, Especially When Problems Arise

What if the customer's horse becomes seriously injured or ill while in the trainer's care? When this happens, the trainer would be wise to communicate promptly with the customer, even if the customer already gave the trainer full discretion to handle everything on his or her behalf.

Communication can benefit everyone and will likely help avoid legal disputes. Generally speaking, the law expects trainers to give "reasonable care" to horses kept in their care, custody, and control. If it turns out that the trainer has, acting on his own, exercised poor judgment and jeopardized the health and well-being of a horse in training, the owner might assert that the horse was denied reasonable care. Under these circumstances, the owner might even seek legal action against the trainer for the loss or devaluation of the trained horse.

Use Written Contracts

A carefully drafted training contract could benefit all parties involved in the training relationship. The training contract can include, *at a minimum*:

- A statement of purpose of the training
- Fees and other payment obligations
- What to do in case of an emergency (who to contact, authorization to take certain actions or spend up to a certain amount in veterinary bills on the owner's behalf, and more)
- Whether the trainer can solicit or accept offers to sell the horse for a given price
- The state whose law applies

Many trainers also insist on other provisions such as releases of liability (where allowed by law), the location for legal disputes, insurance requirements, a one-month evaluation period by the trainer for an established fee, and many others.

Remember How Insurance Applies

Prompt notification of the insurer is a critical prerequisite to coverage under most equine mortality insurance policies. It is critical that trainers know which horses kept under their care have mortality insurance coverage, as well as the insurer's policy numbers and emergency telephone numbers.

Focus on Professionalism

Horse training is a serious service business. The relationship works when *both* parties take their obligations seriously. For the trainer, this means training the horse in good faith, answering phone calls, and being willing to communicate with the customer. For the customer, this means paying the trainer on time and staying mindful of the trainer's busy schedule.

If a Dispute Arises, Think Before Acting or Speaking Out

Trainers should consider seeking legal advice, particularly before taking serious action, such as selling a horse, making demands for payment, or pursuing a lawsuit to collect unpaid fees. Various state laws, such as debt collection practice laws or stablemen's lien laws, could directly impact these efforts.

Also, trainers rushing to court too hastily against their clients might be surprised when confronted, in response, with a counterclaim (a countersuit) brought against them. The client's counterclaim might assert that the trainer somehow violated the training contract and failed to give the horse reasonable care during the training relationship. Regardless of who ultimately wins the case, the cost of legal fees and the amount of disruption to both parties from a lawsuit might be far more than either ever bargained for.

Many disputes arising in the horse training relationship—especially if both parties appear to have claims against each other—can be suitable for resolution through alternative means of dispute resolution, such as mediation. Mediation is a process in which the parties to a dispute agree to allow one or more unbiased persons to serve as a facilitator to help resolve it. The job of a mediator is not to decide who wins or loses. Rather, the mediator encourages both sides to discuss their position and to make an attempt to resolve their dispute. [See *Equine Law & Horse Sense* for a more detailed discussion of mediation.]

Try to End the Relationship Without "Bad Blood"

The fact is, not all trainer/client matches will be successful. When the relationship ends, all accounts between the parties should be promptly settled. Also, both parties should think carefully before acting maliciously or "bad-mouthing" the other; the right of free speech in our country is a constitutionally protected guarantee, but there are legal limits. Even when relationships end on the most bitter terms, where both parties never want to see the other again, they should avoid conditions that could generate claims of slander (spoken defamatory words), libel (written defamatory words), disparagement (defaming a business), illegal interference with the other's business relationships, or others. These situations could force the parties' relationship to continue for a long time—in a courtroom.

HOW TO AVOID COMMON DISPUTES INVOLVING EQUINE LEASES

Over the years, equine leases have been the subject of many disputes in the horse industry. Here are some of them as well as ways that disputes can be avoided.

What is a Lease?

In an equine lease arrangement, one person (the "lessor") allows another person (the "lessee") to use a horse for a certain period of time, under certain conditions, and often for a fee, under satisfactory terms.

Common Disputes And How to Avoid Them

Here are a few problems people have encountered with leases:

- *Person A rides a horse she got from Person B. After Person A has had the horse a year, Person B demands the horse be returned to him. Person A says she bought the horse from Person B, but Person B says she only leased him to Person A.*

Because the parties had completely different understandings of the same transaction, they had to settle their differences through a costly lawsuit. This case forced a judge, who knew nothing about horses, to decide who was telling the truth and whether their arrangement was a sale or a lease.

- *At the end of the lease term, the horse is returned to the lessor in an injured, lame, wormy, underfed, or worn-out condition. Or, while the lease is still in effect, the lessor might learn that the lessee is giving the horse improper or inhumane care and want to immediately end the lease and re-claim the horse.*

In this scenario, the lessor wanted the right to control the quality of care the horse received during the term of the lease. On the other hand, the lessee likely wanted discretion to handle, feed, and care for the horse as the lessee saw fit, without any intervention by the lessor.

- *The lessee might allow a friend to ride the leased horse. When the friend gets hurt, the friend sues both the lessor and the lessee.*

Unfortunately, these problems really happened. A common theme connecting all of them is that the lease arrangements were purely verbal— none of the parties had tried to protect themselves with a carefully written agreement. An effectively written lease contract might have eliminated these and many other problems.

Elements of Effective Leases

With equine-related leases, the parties often have opposite interests. A carefully worded written agreement can seek to accommodate these competing interests.

Every equine-related lease transaction is different. Because of this, no one form contract can work best for everybody, which is why form leases bought from a book are not as helpful as people often think them to be. However, you can use the list below to evaluate your form lease or prepare your information for your lawyer (and probably cut the cost of lease preparation).

A well-written equine lease should include, at a minimum:

- A clear description of the horse involved
- The dates when the lease will begin and end
- Whether the lease can be renewed for another term, and how
- Payments, if any, the lessee must make to the lessor
- How the lessee can use the horse and restrictions, if any, on what the lessee can do with the horse during the term of the lease
- The quality of care (also known as "standard of care") that the lessee must give to the horse
- The lessor's rights, if any, to terminate the lease and re-claim the horse without first resorting to a court of law if he or she believes that the lessee has violated the lease (state laws may govern these types of provisions), or other actions that the lessor may take if the lessee fails to honor his or her obligations. (These kinds of provisions can also include the lessee's rights to receive notice from the lessor of any perceived violations and a time frame in which to resolve them so that the lease can remain in effect)
- Who pays routine veterinary and farrier bills while the lease is in effect
- Who, if anyone, will pay for veterinary attention if the horse should suffer a severe injury or illness (such as a severe cut or colic)

- Who must buy insurance applicable to the horse or its use, such as mortality, major medical, and/or liability insurance

- The lessor will probably want a release of liability (where allowed by law) and an indemnification agreement

- Use taxes, if any are imposed by law, and who will pay them

- An option to use an alternative to the legal system, such as arbitration, to resolve any disputes

- Who will pay the legal fees if a dispute should arise from the lease

If the lessor has the horse insured under a policy of equine insurance, such as a mortality insurance policy, or liability insurance policy, the lessor would be wise to notify his or her insurer to determine whether the leasing arrangement will adversely affect coverage.

Conclusion

While written lease agreements cannot prevent all legal disputes from occurring, they can either eliminate or narrow the grounds of a dispute. In a legal battle, this often can mean a substantial savings of money.

CHAPTER FIVE

SELECTING AND MANAGING AN EQUINE BUSINESS

Selecting the Right Structure for Your Business

Equine industry professionals, just like everybody else doing business, need to select a structure for their business. The options are:

1. Sole Proprietorship

2. General Partnership

3. Limited Partnership

4. Corporation (C-corporation or S-corporation)

5. Limited Liability Company

Types of Structures for your Business

1. Sole Proprietorship

Number of People Required:	One
Benefit:	Easiest to establish
Disadvantage:	Personal liability of the sole proprietor
How to Establish:	Begin doing business, with possible filings

If you operate a business without a corporation or formal business entity, and without partners, you are considered a "sole proprietor." As a sole proprietor, you are personally liable for the debts and liabilities of your business.

Typically, sole proprietors can operate under an assumed name (also called a "fictitious name"). As an example, if Jane Doe wanted to do business under the name of "Happy Trails Riding Stable," she would file in the county where the business is located a "fictitious" or "assumed name" certificate.

The tax laws treat sole proprietors and their businesses as the same. You will need to file a Schedule C (Form 1040) or, in some instances, a Schedule C-EZ, in which you will report your business profits or losses on your individual income tax return.

2. General Partnership (Also Known as a "Co-Partnership")

Number of	
People Required:	Two or more
Benefit:	Easy to establish
Disadvantage:	Personal liability of the partners
How to Establish:	Partnership agreement and file forms

If you and at least one other person carry out a business activity together, you have created a general partnership (also known as a "co-partnership"). The biggest disadvantage is that the general partners are personally liable if someone should sue the partnership for injuries arising from the partnership or its business debts. If you operate the partnership under an assumed name or a fictitious name (such as John Day and Jean Night doing business as "Day & Night Farm") you may be required to secure a Certificate of Co-Partnership or Certificate of Assumed Name. These forms are typically filed in the county where the business is located. The partnership should also set up a bank account under the business name. General partnerships are best established by a written agreement, as explained further in this chapter.

3. Limited Partnership

Number of	
People Required:	Two or more
Benefit:	Limited partners have no personal liability
Disadvantage:	General partners have personal liability
How to Establish:	Partnership agreement and file Certificate of Limited Partnership forms with the state

A limited partnership has two kinds of partners—*general partners* and *limited partners*. The general partner(s) manage the partnership's business. The limited partners do not. Unlike general partners, who face unlimited personal liability for the liabilities and obligations of the partnership, the most the limited partners stand to lose is what they invested in the partnership.

Limited partnerships cannot be created informally. They require partnership agreements and filings with the state. Also, a limited partnership needs its own separate bank account for the business it conducts. Because of these complexities, anyone considering a limited partnership should consult with legal counsel.

4. Corporation (C-corporation or S-corporation)

Number of People Required:	One or more
Benefit:	No personal liability of the shareholders
Disadvantage:	Requires separate banking, issuance of stock, and other filings and formalities
How to Establish:	File Articles of Incorporation with the state of incorporation

The main benefit of a corporation is that its shareholders are protected from liabilities that may arise out of the corporation's business operations. This means that if an incorporated riding instructor is sued by a student who was injured in a riding lesson, the instructor's corporation would be the proper party to the lawsuit and the corporation's assets would be used to pay off a judgment.

A corporation's biggest disadvantage is that its existence depends on following basic formalities (discussed in this chapter) and filing several forms with the state. For example, before doing business, the corporation must file Articles of Incorporation with the state. Corporations also need to hold directors meetings, shareholder meetings, draft Corporate By-Laws and annual meeting minutes, and submit filings to the state of incorporation each year.

Below is a brief summary of the two different types of corporations – C corporation and S corporation. All corporations are C corporations unless they make appropriate and timely filings with the IRS to elect S-corporation status.

C-CORPORATION	**S-CORPORATION**
ADVANTAGES	
No personal liability of shareholders	No personal liability of shareholders; only the shareholders taxed on profits
DISADVANTAGES	
Corporation pays taxes on profits; shareholders pay taxes on distributed money. **Result:** double taxation	Extra filings with the IRS; restrictions on who and how many people can be shareholders

continued on next page

C-CORPORATION	S-CORPORATION
KEY FEATURES	
• Only structure available for corporations with over 75 shareholders and/or with non-U.S. citizen shareholders • Pays corporate taxes based on profits • May distribute money (called "dividends") to its shareholders • Shareholders pay taxes on their dividends	• To create an S corporation, the entity must file a Form 2553 with the IRS within (1) 75 days from the time the corporation first has shareholders, assets, or starts doing business; or (2) before March 15 each year thereafter • No more than 75 shareholders total; all shareholders must be U.S. citizens; other restrictions may apply • Tax obligations are passed through from the corporation to its shareholders

5. Limited Liability Company (LLC)

Number of People Required: One or more (Two or more in some states)

Benefit: No personal liability of the owners (members); members are typically taxed as if they are partners

Disadvantage: Harder to set up than a corporation; could require greater legal expense to set up

How to Establish: File Articles of Organization with the state of formation, and have an operating agreement

The limited liability company ("LLC") is considered to be a cross between a partnership and an S corporation. Much like a corporation, the owners (members) of an LLC are not personally liable for the LLC's obligations. However, an LLC is typically taxed as a partnership (unless the LLC files a special election with the Internal Revenue Service to choose non-partnership taxation). This means that income, credits, losses, and deductions flow through to the individual members of the LLC. Most states now allow single-member LLCs.

102

Establishing an LLC requires filing Articles of Organization and having an operating agreement if there is more than one member (owner) of the LLC. Just like the other formally established business structures, the LLC must have its own separate bank account.

The LLC entity is especially desirable for entities that, by virtue of their size (more than 75 owners/members) or composition (some non-US resident owners/members) do not qualify for S-corporation status.

BUSINESS TIPS FOR SELF-EMPLOYED EQUINE PROFESSIONALS

Horse trainers, riding instructors, show managers, breeders, haulers and boarding stable owners—what do these people have in common? They are usually referred to as "equine professionals," and they are usually self-employed. They also have in common that they usually work at full capacity—at the barn early and retiring very late into the night after the last customer has left and the last horse is checked. Working harder to make more money is not really an option.

There is a major difference between working *harder* and working *smarter*. If you are an equine professional, this section will give you tips for working smarter. Working smarter may include:

- Taking advantage of Federal and state government resources
- Belonging to associations
- Two little known but important business filings
- Tax payments you may need to make
- Money-saving tax benefits and deductions
- How you can plan for the future with your own self-employed pension
- Two types of insurance that professionals cannot afford to overlook

Federal Government Resources You Need to Know

Put your tax dollars to work for you. The Federal government offers a wide variety of programs, services, and information for small businesses, and equine professionals have to start looking at themselves as a small business. Many of these resources are available through the internet, and several are free. Here are some:

The U.S. Small Business Administration ("SBA"). The SBA is an independent federal agency that was created to, among other things, "aid, counsel, assist and protect the interests of small-business concerns." The SBA offers loan guarantee programs and numerous other services for those who qualify. It can be reached at (800) 827-5722 or (800) U-ASK-SBA. The SBA is also on the world wide web at http:/

/www.sba.gov/. Its electronic bulletin board is on the internet at http://www.ecrc.ctc.com.

The U.S. Business Advisor. This service offers general information about assistance offered by the federal government and news of interest to the business community. Contact it at http://www.business.gov/.

U.S. Chamber of Commerce. Small business owners can contact the U.S. Chamber of Commerce at (202) 659-6000. Its web site is: http://www.uschamber.org/.

Your Congressman or Congresswoman. If you have questions about United States government resources, contact your United States Representative in Washington, D.C., at his or her local office. Very likely, your local government office can help you reach him or her. Or, contact the U.S. Capitol operator at (202) 224-3121.

State Government Resources That Can Benefit Your Business

In addition, here are other resources available from or within your state:

State Chamber of Commerce. Your state likely has a Chamber of Commerce. This organization usually gives information on business development resources in the state; or, it can refer you to regional chamber of commerce locations near you.

Regional Chamber of Commerce. Regions within your state might offer their own chambers of commerce, which promote businesses. These groups offer you the chance to meet other business owners in your community and let them learn about you.

State Department of Agriculture. Many states have programs, such as rural development programs, that could benefit your business. Contact your agriculture department.

To learn more about small business resources, programs, and services that are available within your state, contact the U.S. Government Printing Office at (202) 512-1800 and request its book called *The States and Small Business: A Directory of Programs and Activities* (Government Printing Office stock number 045-000-00266-7).

Join Up With Associations

Across the country thousands of horse-related associations exist. They range from the local 4-H club to regional breed-oriented groups to national associations (such as the American Horse Shows Association or American Quarter Horse Association).

Association membership *does* have its privileges. These groups offer you the chance to get to know others and let them learn about you and your business. This can greatly expand your client base as the people you meet bring you business and refer others to you.

In addition, here are some of the other benefits that associations offer:

- Discounts on equipment ranging from helmets and riding gear to office supplies
- Discounts on airfare, hotel, and automobile rentals
- Credit cards available to association members with discounted interest rates and often no annual fee
- Health insurance discounts and benefit plans for employees
- Web-site hosting
- Long-distance telephone service discounts
- Internet access discounts
- Annual conventions and expos, which offer information on important developments affecting your business as well as the chance to meet others
- Liability insurance discounts

Two Important Business Filings
That Are Often Overlooked by Small Businesses

Remember to register your business name. If you are a sole proprietor or a partnership and are doing business under a name different from your own, you will need to file for a "fictitious" or "assumed" name certificate. This certificate lets the public know the true owner of your business. Depending on your form of business and state requirements, you will direct your application to your county government.

Get a business license, if required by law. Equine professionals need to comply with state and local licensing requirements. Some states, such as California, require almost all businesses to be licensed. Many states, such as Michigan, require stables to be licensed. Massachusetts requires riding instructors to be licensed.

Tax Payments You May Need to Make

Self-employment taxes. As of August 1999, the Federal government requires all self-employed individuals to pay a self-employment tax. This tax combines the Social Security and Medicare tax for these individuals. The self-employment tax rate (as of August 1999) was approximately 15.3% (which combines a 12.4% Social Security tax and a 2.9% Medicare tax) of the first $72,600, and a tax of 2.9% on income over that amount. For more information on self-employment taxes, contact the Internal Revenue Service (IRS) to receive *Information on Self-Employment Tax* (IRS Publication 553). For more information on this and other federal taxes, check your local phone book for the number of an IRS office, or visit the IRS web site at http://www.irs.ustreas.gov/.

Other tax requirements. Depending on your business structure, whether you have employees, and the law that applies, you may be required to pay personal property taxes (these taxes are assessed by your local government based on the value of certain of your personal belongings and equipment) and unemployment taxes. Discuss these and other taxes with your accountant.

Tax Benefits and Deductions That Can Save You Money

The good news is that self-employed equine professionals may be entitled to many tax deductions. Here are some of them:

Home office deduction. Especially for equine professionals who do their record-keeping, office work, billing, client meetings, and horse buying and selling communications through their home, the home office deduction could be valuable. This deduction applies to those who live in houses, apartments, condos, or even mobile homes or boats.

If you qualify for the home office deduction, you can deduct from your taxes a portion of your expenses for rent, home insurance, utilities, and home repairs. For more information, contact the IRS to get its publication called *Business Use of Your Home* (IRS Publication 587) or *Expenses for Business Use of Your Home* (IRS Form 8829). Or, visit the IRS web site at http://www.irs.ustreas.gov/.

Meals and entertainment expenses. Under limited circumstances, you might be able to deduct certain meal and entertainment expenses.

Auto expenses. Most equine professionals consider their trucks to be their business partners. You might be legally permitted to deduct from your taxes a portion of your truck and trailer expenses, even gasoline and maintenance, as long as the expenses are sufficiently related to your business.

Plan For Your Future
With a Self-Employed Pension (SEP)

Businesses often give their employees retirement savings programs. Equine professionals can give themselves these benefits, too, if they set up a Self-Employed Pension (SEP-IRA).

SEP-IRAs are easy to set up, and you do not even need to file forms with the IRS. As of August 1999, you can invest up to 13.04% of your earnings each year (current tax laws actually specify 15% as the maximum investment, but tax experts say that the contribution actually calculates to 13.04%), with a maximum investment of $24,000 annually.

Self-employed pensions offer major tax benefits. Your accountant can discuss the details with you. For more information, contact the IRS about receiving two booklets: *Self Employed Retirement Plans* (IRS Publication 560) and/or *Individual Retirement Accounts* (IRS Publication 590).

Remember to Pay Yourself

Companies usually pay their workers on a regular basis. If you are self-employed, "pay day" is when you set it. Investing your profits back into your business can make sense, when needed. Paying yourself makes good sense, too.

Important Insurance for Equine Professionals

Health insurance. If you are self-employed, you must pay for your own health insurance. Because of the inherent risks associated with working around horses, it makes good sense for self-employed equine professionals to have health insurance in effect at all times.

Disability Income Insurance. Self-employed professionals who derive all of their income from equine activities (such as riding instructors) should consider buying disability insurance. If illness or injury renders the professional unable to work, this insurance would replace a portion of his or her lost income for a certain period of time.

Liability insurance. Equine professionals, regardless of the structure in which they do business, should buy proper liability insurance. The types of liability insurance coverages of special interest to equine professionals, depending on their operations, include:

- Commercial General Liability Insurance
- Care, Custody, and Control Insurance
- Equine Professional Liability Insurance

If you are a sole proprietor or a general partner in an equine business, the risk of your own personal liability gives you a powerful incentive to buy liability insurance with the highest limits you can afford. [Insurance is covered in Chapter Ten of this book, as well as in *Equine Law & Horse Sense*.]

Will Your Corporation Limit Your Personal Liability? Nine Suggestions for Taking Your Corporation Seriously So That Others Will, too

Corporations are desirable in horse industry businesses because they can serve as a liability shield. That is, people running the corporation are typically not subject to personal liability if the corporation incurs debts and liabilities from its business activities. This protection can be especially desirable if your equine business faces the risk of a lawsuit that could exceed the highest liability insurance limits.

How to Avoid Personal Liability

Every small business should be aware of "piercing the corporate veil." This is a legal phrase that means the court disregards your corporation—as if it never existed—and tries to hold you, its shareholder, *personally* liable for the corporation's debts or obligations.

"Piercing the corporate veil" challenges are not common, but they can happen if you fail to treat your corporation as a corporation. By securing good professional advice and following the suggestions that follow, however, you will help prevent an attempt to hold you personally liable for your corporation's debts and liabilities. Or, if challenges do occur, you will help your corporation emerge victorious.

1. Get a Federal Employer Identification Number

Every corporation needs a Federal Employer Identification Number (known as a "FEIN"or "EIN") before doing business. This is comparable to your Social Security number. The FEIN is required before opening a bank account, filing a corporate tax return, sending business invoices, making a tax deposit, and, of course, hiring employees. The Internal Revenue Service (IRS) application for a FEIN is Form SS-4, Application for an Employer Identification Number. After you submit the application form by mail or fax, the IRS will issue the FEIN to your corporation. The IRS may even accept an application by phone using the TELE-TIN service offered by the IRS. Check your local phone book for the number of the IRS Service Center that handles your region of the country.

2. Do Separate Banking for the Corporation

In the eyes of the law, your corporation is separate from you, and you should treat your corporation as a separate entity, which means keeping business money and personal money separate. Business owners who commingle their personal and corporate funds are especially at risk of a "piercing the corporate veil" legal challenge. Consequently, any business-related funds passing through the corporation should be paid by or deposited into the corporate bank accounts, not your own personal bank accounts. This applies to expenses, such as a boarding stable's payments to the feed store, as well as income, such as a riding instructor's lesson income. The Internal Revenue Service (IRS) does not absolutely require that you deposit all business income into a bank account, but it is important to be sure that income attributable to the business gets reported as business income.

Also, do not pay personal expenses with corporation money. The act of using corporate funds to pay the personal debts of its proprietors can also prompt a "piercing the corporate veil" challenge.

3. Keep the Corporation's Accounts Reasonably Well Funded (Capitalized)

Proper maintenance of a corporation requires keeping the corporation's bank accounts funded with reasonably sufficient funds to meet expected debts. This does not mean a huge stockpile of money. Rather, it means, for example, that your operation as an incorporated riding instructor who pays over $500 a month to lease an equine facility would be suspicious if you only maintained a constant bank balance of $100.

4. Operate the Business Under the Corporate Name
or
A Properly Established Fictitious Name
of the Corporation

What if your corporation does business under another name that differs from the corporation's name? The other name is called a "fictitious" or "assumed" name. Businesses can establish assumed names, whether or not they are incorporated. Consequently, if your corporation is "XYZ, Inc.," and if the state has approved your papers formally requesting to transact business under the assumed name of "Morningstar Farms," you can conduct your business under either name.

Before your corporation operates under an assumed name, however, make sure that you have first submitted a proper filing with the state of the incorporation. The state will keep records of the corporation's assumed name and typically will help prevent the problem of another corporation in that state operating under the same name.

5. File Annual Reports With the State

Virtually all states require corporations and some other entities (such as Limited Liability Companies) to file annual reports with the appropriate state entity as a condition to maintaining their status; your state may call this entity the Secretary of State or Department of Commerce. Each state provides a special form for the report and sets a deadline for the corporation to return it, together with a small filing fee. Annual reports generally include (1) names and addresses of the corporation's officers and directors, and (2) the name and address of the corporation's designated Registered Agent. (A Registered Agent is the one designated to receive certain communications and lawsuit papers on behalf of the corporation.) In addition, some states require the corporation to file, along with its annual report, a balance sheet that summarizes the corporation's assets and liabilities during a given time period, and states the number of corporate shares issued to shareholders.

Busy equine businesses cannot afford to miss the annual report filing requirement. In fact, under the laws of most states, corporations that neglect to file their annual reports over a designated period of time risk having their corporate authority revoked altogether.

6. Keep Corporate Minutes and Records

The laws of every state require corporations to maintain records of important corporate activities. For example, you will be required to keep a written record of significant transactions that include, *at a minimum*, bank loan documents, minutes of shareholder meetings, elections of corporate officers and directors, establishment or amendment of corporate by-laws, and lists of officers and directors' names and addresses. These records are considered internal documents, and states typically do not require that you file them with state offices.

Corporations hold meetings of their shareholders and board of directors; the notes or memoranda of what takes place at these meetings are called "minutes." Minutes of shareholders and directors meetings can include:

- Date, time, and place of meeting
- Names of persons attending the meeting
- Names of those who attended only a portion of the meeting and what portion(s) they attended or missed

- Whether a quorum (typically, a majority) of the board of directors was present

- Action taken. (Example: the board agreed to prepay a loan to ABC Corporation, the shareholders elected directors, the directors elected officers, etc.)

Keep corporate records and minutes in a handy location, such as in specially labeled binders or folders, and maintain them for as long as the corporation stays in existence.

7. Sign Contracts Properly

How does the corporation represent itself to the public? Do people with whom the corporation does business know that they are dealing with a corporation and not you as an individual?

If your incorporated stable uses contracts, such as sales and boarding contracts, which nowhere mention the corporation, this might prompt someone's attempt to impose personal liability on you as the stable's owner. To avoid this problem, and to reaffirm that the entity is a corporation, corporate contracts should specifically name the corporation and identify the status of the one who has signed the contract on behalf of the corporation. For example:

Sunny Days Farm, Inc.

By: _____
Jane Doe, President

8. Stay Adequately Insured

Equine businesses that assume they are protected by a business owner's basic homeowner's insurance policy could be making a very costly mistake. Liability insurance policies usually exclude coverage for claims arising from a "business pursuit" of the one insured. This means, for example, that if someone is hurt while engaging in a business activity you provide—such as giving a paid riding lesson or boarding a horse for a fee—the standard homeowner's insurance policy will likely *not* protect your business in the event that a claim or suit is filed. It typically takes a policy of "commercial general liability" insurance to protect a business in this setting.

When buying business-related insurance, make sure to name the corporation as an insured party. Also, consider including yourself and others affiliated with you as "additional named insureds" on the policy. Discuss this option with your insurance agent or lawyer.

9. Get a Business License (If Required By Law)

Some states require certain professionals, such as stables or riding instructors, to be licensed. If your state's licensing requirements involve naming the business on the license document, and if the license can be issued to a business rather than to an individual, make sure that the corporation's name appears.

Conclusion

In conclusion, please keep these concepts in mind:

1. Remember to run your corporation like a corporation—regardless of whether it is owned and operated by one person or there are several people involved. Use your business name when doing business, and put business money in a business bank account.

2. For the busy equine business, corporate filing deadlines can easily be missed, and the possibility always exists that mailings could be misplaced or lost in the mail. Plan ahead by keeping a calendar with flagged reminders so that your business never misses a filing requirement or deadline.

3. Keep important papers in a safe place. Make sure to organize your corporate minutes, by-laws, and records in a folder or binder, and store them for as long as the corporation exists.

4. Remember that your corporation is not legally official until the state has accepted your corporate filings, approved the corporate name and assumed name, and received the required filing fees. Before promoting or using a corporate name or assumed name, contact the state to determine whether another corporation, through its filings, has already reserved the right to do business under that name.

YOU'RE AN EQUINE PARTNERSHIP—NOW WHAT?

Over coffee one day, Sam and Paula agreed to set up a brand new equine business. Each of them will give something of value. Paula, who has no horse training expertise, will lend the use of her horse farm and several of her well-bred, but untrained, horses. Sam, a horse trainer, will lend his time conditioning, training, and racing Paula's horses. Paula and Sam agree that they will later sell off the partnership's horses and split all profits 50-50. They shake hands on the deal, with no written contract.

In the horse industry, people often set up partnerships much like Sam and Paula did. However, when set up without a carefully written partnership agreement, a partnership arrangement creates fertile ground for many disputes. For example:

- Sam might sign a purchase agreement on behalf of the partnership for an expensive new horse trailer, even if he and Paula agreed that he could not buy trailers, and both partners would likely be bound by his purchase (and personally liable to pay the debt if the partnership has no money).

- While Sam exercises one of the partnership's horses at the track, the horse might hurt someone passing by. Paula, even though she has never trained a horse in her life, can be sued because she is a partner in the business.

- After Sam has spent months of his time training the partnership's horses, Paula might want to call the deal off and, to this end, try to re-claim the horses she gave to the partnership.

As their arrangement falls apart, Sam and Paula learn that they should have looked at their relationship as a partnership business, not just a joint project, because partnership laws do apply to them. In this section, you will learn:

- What is a partnership, and types of partnerships
- Risks associated with belonging to a partnership

- Benefits of a well-written contract
- Elements of a written partnership contract
- Documents and government filings that partnerships generally file

Types of Partnerships

General partnership (also called a "Co-Partnership"). In the eyes of the law, you have created a general partnership if you and at least one other person carry out a business activity together. As one reliable legal source puts it, a general partnership is "an association of two or more persons to carry on as co-owners of a business for profit." [Source: Uniform Partnership Act (UPA), Section 6(1).]

Joint venture. A joint venture is a type of partnership that is created for a limited or specific purpose. For example, joint ventures are sometimes established around breeding stallions, in which two people agree to promote a stallion to the public and share income from stud fees. Joint ventures are governed by basic partnership law.

Limited Partnership. A limited partnership is a partnership that has two kinds of partners—*general partners* and *limited partners*. The general partners are much like Sam and Paula, and generally they manage the partnership's business. The benefit for limited partners is that they are typically not involved in running the business. Also, unlike general partners, who face unlimited personal liability for the unpaid debts and obligations of the partnership, limited partners only stand to lose what they invested in the partnership.

Limited partnerships cannot be created informally. They require special contracts and special filings with the state and may also be subject to federal and state securities laws (complex laws that regulate several types of arrangements in which people invest money or something of value). Because of these complexities and government regulations, anyone considering a limited partnership should consult with legal counsel.

How is a Partnership Taxed?

Each individual partner is taxed on his or her allocated share of the profits or losses, but the partnership will have to file an informational tax return with the government. Partnerships, just like other businesses, may be required to pay other taxes, such as payroll and unemployment taxes.

Risks

In any general partnership, each partner is personally and individually liable for the legal obligations that the partnership cannot pay, such as debts and liabilities. In the example above, if Sam purchases an expensive horse trailer—even though he and Paula specifically agreed that he could not make this purchase—the partnership is bound by this purchase because it was made within the course of the partnership's business. If the partnership does not have the money to pay for the trailer, the trailer seller can seek the money from both Sam and Paula's personal assets.

On the other hand, if a partner encounters debts in his or her personal, non-partnership matters, the partnership is not legally responsible for paying those debts. For example, if Paula fails to pay her credit card bill, the credit card company cannot legally claim the partnerships profits, including Sam's share. The company could, however, seek to claim Paula's share of the profits.

Benefits of a Written Agreement

Partnerships arranged through a handshake and a verbal understanding can, in many cases, be legal. However, should a dispute ever arise between the partners, it will be difficult to prove the terms of an agreement—or even that a partnership agreement existed.

Equine business pursuits are often carried out in a way that makes partnership status unclear. For example, an unincorporated riding instructor might consider her assistant an employee, while the assistant believes that she is a partner in the business. Or, a horse trainer might believe that he is in partnership with his client when the two strike a deal to waive training fees in exchange for a share of the prize money or profits if the horse later sells. These misunderstandings can be avoided if the parties reduce their arrangement to a carefully written agreement.

Possible Elements of
a Written Partnership Agreement

A written agreement for a general partnership can include, *at a minimum*, the following elements:

- *Name, purpose, and location of the partnership.* A partnership can be created for any purpose permitted by law. A carefully worded agreement can specify the name under which the partnership will transact business, its purpose and location where it will transact business.

116

- *Identities of each the partners.* State the names and addresses of each partner.

- *What each partner is contributing to the venture.* The agreement can specify, for example, the amount of cash paid by each partner, name(s) and descriptions of each horse contributed to the partnership by each partner, and each horse's market value. The agreement can also state whether any partner has contributed equipment, property, or services.

- *What (if anything) each partner must contribute to the partnership in the future.*

- *Percentage ownership of the partners.* Will all partners share equally in the ownership? Or, will one partner own 75% of the business and the three other partners split the remaining 25%? The partnership agreement can also indicate that each partner's voting rights will be equal to his or her percentage of ownership.

- *Management.* The partnership agreement can specify, for example, whether the partners will share equally in the partnership's management; or, the agreement can delegate management authority to one of the partners or someone else. The partnership agreement could also specify partnership meetings for the partners to discuss partnership business.

- *Limitations on what the partners can do.* Many partnership agreements clearly specify that a partner cannot do certain things without the prior written consent of all partners, such as borrow money, make a loan, guarantee payment of a debt, transfer or sell partnership assets, hire employees, or buy or lease property.

- *Insurance.* The partnership agreement can specify that the partnership must purchase certain types of insurance. Insurance can range from (1) public liability insurance designed to protect the partnership and its members, to (2) life, medical, dental, disability, hospital, or other insurance for the benefit of the partnership or the individual partners.

- *Exclusivity.* If a busy horse trainer agrees to devote some of his or her time to training horses belonging to a partnership but wants to be free to train other customers' horses, as well, the trainer would be wise to specify this in the contract. The contract can acknowledge that the trainer is devoting some, but not all, of his or her time to the partnership. Alternatively, other partners, who expect a firm commitment of time from the trainer, would be wise to insist on language that sets forth a minimum number of hours that the trainer will devote to the partnership's business. Some partnership agreements include covenants not to compete (where allowed by law), which would seek to prevent a departing trainer/partner from engaging in a similar business pursuit within a certain distance from the partnership's place of business and for a set span of months or years.

- *Profits and losses.* The partnership agreement can specify if the partners will share equally in the partnership's profits and losses according to the individual partner's percentage of ownership.

- *When partnership profits will be distributed.* The partnership agreement can create a definition for what qualifies as "excess funds" and provide a timetable for when the partners can share any of these funds.

- *Banking.* The partnership agreement can designate banks for business accounts and can specify whose signatures will be needed for withdrawals or bank fund transfers.

- *How the partnership can terminate.* Partnerships, like marriages, can fail. This fact alone should encourage partnerships to include in their written contracts procedures through which they can officially end the partnership. One example is that the partners can plan now for a price with which a departing partner's interest in the partnership can be bought out, or a formula to determine a buy-out price.

- *How a partner can be expelled.* The agreement can address the circumstances under which a partner can be expelled, and what will happen if the partnership pursues this option.

- *Admission of new partners.* The agreement can address whether a partner can assign his or her partnership interest to someone else. For example, maybe Paula wants the right to transfer her interest in the partnership to her son. The agreement can also cover procedures in the event that someone seeks to join the partnership.

- *Designated addresses and methods to receive notices regarding partnership business.* The partnership agreement can specify the proper addresses and even fax and e-mail addresses where partnership notices can be sent to each partner.

- *How disputes will be resolved.* If the partners agree now that arbitration or mediation can be utilized to resolve disputes, the agreement would be wise to specify this now.

- *Governing law.* The agreement can specify what state's law governs the agreement and where to file legal proceedings.

Other Partnership Documents

Other than the written partnership agreement that the partners may draft to govern themselves, a partnership might be required to send paperwork to the federal, state, or local government, such as:

- *Federal Employer Identification Number* ("FEIN"or "EIN"). This would be required before hiring employees.

- *Assumed Name or "Fictitious Name" filings.* A general partnership may be required to submit a proper filing, usually at the county level, of the name under which it is transacting business.

- *Certificate of Limited Partnership.* For limited partnerships, the Secretary of State or Department of Commerce require a Certificate of Limited Partnership filing (or similar filing to reflect the limited partnership's existence).

- *Sales Tax Permits.* If the partnership will be selling goods, such as saddle pads or clothing, it may be required to apply for a state resale permit.

CHAPTER SIX

LAND USE
AND ZONING ISSUES

WHAT IS HORSE-FRIENDLY ZONING?

Zoning battles are *very* serious, especially for those who enjoy horses. In the new millennium, zoning battles threaten to become more frequent as large numbers of people move to rural areas to escape city life. Unfortunately for those with horses, the new neighbors do not always appreciate the realities of life near horses. Conflict sometimes results when the new neighbors try to legislate horses out of the community by changing the zoning or land use laws.

Here are examples of some battles:

- The municipality may be considering new zoning classifications or restrictions that will have the effect of lowering the number of horses allowed on each acre of land.

- To make room for new subdivisions and shopping centers, the community will try to re-zone spacious bridle paths to allow for different uses of this land.

To succeed in a zoning-related conflict often requires intense planning, team work, and a general understanding of the zoning process. This section begins by answering these basic questions:

- What is zoning?
- Which government bodies plan and pass zoning ordinances?
- What are typical features found in a zoning ordinance?

What is Zoning?

Cities, villages, and townships (sometimes called "municipalities") have the power to enact regulations that affect and are enforceable within their territorial bounds. These regulations are known as "ordinances." Ordinances that regulate the use of land and buildings involve "zoning."

Zoning, by its very nature, tells you what you can and cannot do on your land. People with horses often are outraged that anyone would tell them how many horses they can have on their land or where they must put their barns. But someone else—who has lived next to a farm housing too many horses and too much dust, noise, manure, and too many flies—will tell you that setting limits is very important for the quality of life in the area and the well-being of the horses.

Around the early 1900s, as our society became mechanized, communities began enacting zoning ordinances, mainly to control congested areas. Over time, however, numerous other reasons have prompted zoning ordinances. For example, ordinances have been enacted to stabilize property values, regulate population density, avoid conflicting land uses between neighboring properties, reduce fire hazards and plan the community's land use needs well into the years ahead.

The goal of zoning and land use ordinances is generally to protect the public's health, safety, and welfare; zoning ordinances typically follow the community's broad land use plan or "master plan." The master plan is a written document kept on file with the local government.

Who Plans and Passes Zoning Ordinances?

The local legislative body that votes to adopt a new zoning ordinance is not necessarily the one that writes it. Rather, in many communities the local government delegates much of the work of ordinance drafting and review to a sub-committee known as a zoning or planning board or commission.

The zoning or planning board or commission, before it formally recommends new or changed zoning ordinances to the local legislative body, will first evaluate the need for the ordinance and invite public involvement through notice procedures established by law. After that, the zoning or planning board or commission prepares a draft ordinance for public comment at a hearing.

At the conclusion of the hearing, the zoning or planning board or commission will vote on whether to recommend that the municipal government adopt the new or changed ordinance. If the group votes "yes," the proposed ordinance moves on to the municipality's governing body. Before that body votes to adopt or reject a proposed ordinance, however, one or more public hearings will take place.

Features of a Zoning Ordinance— Horse Friendly or Not?

A typical zoning ordinance categorizes the municipality into zones (such as A-1 for agricultural uses, A-2 for agricultural and rural residential uses, and many others) and then describes what land uses are permitted or prohibited within each classified zone. Zoning ordinances can regulate other provisions and aspects of land use, as well.

Below are features sometimes found in horse-related zoning ordinances that can affect whether or not they are horse-friendly.

- Lot sizes needed for a family dwelling
- Maximum number of horses per acre
- Maximum number of buildings that can be allowed on a lot
- Setback restrictions for fencing and barns (typically specifying the minimum distance that you can place a building, fence, or arena from your property line or street)
- Height limits or minimums for structures and fences on the lot
- Restrictions on the percentage of a lot that can be covered by buildings or structures
- "Horse permits" (requiring horse owners to complete, sometimes annually, an application; the application may require a filing fee, and in some cases adjacent landowners may even have the opportunity to challenge issuance of the permit)
- Equestrian district/agricultural zoning with large lot sizes set as minimums
- Whether and where horses can be stabled or used for business purposes such as boarding, training, lessons, or others
- Permitted fencing materials, types, and heights

Certainly, people will differ on what they find "horse-friendly" based on the number of horses they own and the type of land use they plan. You decide what features are best for you.

HOW TO BUY HORSE-FRIENDLY REAL ESTATE WITHOUT BUYING A LAND USE LAWSUIT

Imagine spending many thousands—or even millions—of dollars to buy land with the goal of stabling your horses on it, only to learn after the fact that the zoning regulations forbid the use you planned. Even worse, imagine having to invest heavily in legal fees, abandon your plans, or sell the property because your dreams cannot become reality.

Many people have gone through the expense and emotional cost of that happening. With careful planning, it will not happen to you. This section covers some of the many precautions worth taking before you buy property, including:

- Questions to ask before you buy property
- Laws and ordinances worth checking
- How to give yourself sufficient time to examine the laws, while accommodating an impatient seller

Why Pay Attention to Zoning and Land Use Regulations?

Local land use laws differ greatly when it comes to horses and livestock. There simply can never be a guarantee that one city's land use rules will be the same as another's. Because of this, if you buy property with an equine-related purpose in mind (such as boarding, breeding, giving lessons, training, or even just keeping your own backyard horse), you should investigate the local government's land use restrictions and ordinances (ordinances are local laws affecting municipalities, such as villages, cities, or townships). Never assume that they will be favorable.

Ordinances are usually written by people who know nothing about horses, and, consequently, they sometimes do not make sense to horse people. A case in point—the local government in this author's neighborhood wanted to pass an ordinance *banning* electric fencing for horses. That idea was dropped after several horse owners gently explained to local government leaders that electrified fence wires do not deliver deadly shocks and are a common way of helping keep horses in their pastures.

126

Some Questions to Ask

Before you buy property with the goal of stabling horses on it, do your homework. Do not sign contracts or part with your money until you get clear, reliable, and preferably *written* answers to the following questions:

What is the property's zoning classification? Inspecting the property to see its present use will tell little about its permitted *future* use. Conflict may be waiting to happen if, for example, you buy property which has housed the seller's own horses, but you later try to transform it into a business for breeding, boarding, or training. If the property was zoned for residential or agricultural purposes, the municipality—correctly or not—might classify your planned use as "commercial" and assert that it runs afoul of the zoning laws.

How do the local ordinances affect fencing? If the local ordinances require wood fencing only, this will ruin your plans to install metal, mesh, or polymer fencing. To override this legally, you are virtually assured a trip to your community's zoning board of appeals, with no guarantee of success. Expect to see that body, too, if the fencing you plan runs afoul of height and set-back restrictions.

Will the property's size and configuration allow you to add new structures, such as another residence, manager's residence, new barns or an indoor arena, while staying in compliance with zoning ordinances and restrictions? If the answer is no, get very reliable assurances that the municipality will ultimately approve your building plans. Consider hiring a knowledgeable lawyer to advise you of your chances of winning, if you must sue the municipality to get your plans approved.

If the municipality or state has manure-disposal restrictions, are they acceptable to you? In many states, the department of agriculture has issued manure disposal regulations. Ignoring these requirements can be costly. Your operating costs will increase substantially if, for example, you are prevented from spreading or piling manure on the land.

Laws and Ordinances Worth Checking

Before you buy property, secure a copy of the ordinances or laws that affect your planned uses of the land. Here are examples of some:

- Horse ordinances
- Large animal ordinances
- Farm animal ordinances
- Fencing ordinances

- If you plan to run a business, ordinances, if any, that affect animal-related *commercial* uses

Read the ordinances *very* carefully. Find out if they allow, or destroy, your plans. Also, find out whether the state or local government is considering any proposed changes to the laws or ordinances that might take effect after you buy the land.

How to Give Yourself Sufficient Time to Examine the Laws, While Accommodating an Impatient Seller

Getting laws takes time; reading them takes even more time. The seller might be unwilling to wait while you satisfy yourself that the local and state laws work in your favor. With this in mind, consider these ideas:

Include carefully worded contingencies in your offer of purchase. If buying horse-friendly property matters to you, make sure that your offer of purchase specifies that the closing (the date all sales paperwork is signed and the money changes hands) is contingent (dependent) upon you, the buyer, being satisfied that applicable zoning requirements, land use requirements, and laws support your planned use of the land. Your offer can also state that if you are not satisfied, your offer is effectively withdrawn.

If the seller will not accept your contingencies, consider other arrangements. Especially if they want their property sold as quickly as possible, sellers of real estate might reject the contingencies, described above, if you propose them. The seller has good reason for concern; if you are unhappy with the laws and back out of the deal, the seller will have lost valuable time that would otherwise have been spent finding the right buyer. You (the buyer) might want to propose alternative arrangements. For example, your offer of purchase document could set an absolute deadline when you must tell the seller of your satisfaction (or dissatisfaction) with the local zoning and land use laws. Or, you can consider negotiating a *right of first refusal* contract involving the property (a contract stating that if the seller receives a good-faith offer from someone else, the seller will give you an opportunity to match the offer, or beat it, to become the buyer). Your lawyer or real estate agent can discuss these options with you.

Conclusion

For many of us in the horse industry, buying real estate for a home and horse facility is a life-long dream. Without advance planning, that dream could turn into a nightmare, with lengthy, costly lawsuits and an uncertain outcome. Planning ahead before you buy, and seeking out professional help when needed, can make all the difference.

Horse-related Zoning Battles—How to Launch a Strategy So That *Everybody* Wins

Zoning battles can arise in any community. Sometimes they originate from the local government, which might want to change the laws to make it harder to stable horses. Or, you might bring your own matter before a local zoning board.

Here are some examples of zoning battles:

Prompted by a neighboring property owner, the local government might propose a land use change that adversely affects your property. The municipality or property owners within it can propose changes to the way land in the community can be used. Sometimes, proposals try to make it more difficult to keep horses (although horse supporters can always seek changes through their local governments to make zoning favorable to horses). Other times, horses become an unintended casualty of other proposals, such as when a developer petitions to re-zone certain property, formerly used as riding trails, to allow construction of new subdivisions, shopping centers or facilities.

Variances. What if you want to expand your barn, but your plans would run afoul of a set-back restriction requiring at least a 50-foot distance from the barn to the edge of your property? Even though your proposal would violate the law, you still can ask for a variance. Municipalities differ on how a variance can be sought, but variances are typically issued through entities known as the Zoning Board of Appeals or board of adjustment. This body functions to review special matters and hardship cases, and it has the power to recommend officially that the property owner may deviate from the black-letter language of the ordinance. This is most likely to happen if the deviation (the change from the rule) is minor and the existing ordinance would work a hardship or other difficulty on the property owner.

Before the hearing on a variance, the municipality will give notice to owners of property located within a certain distance from your lot. The notice will advise the nearby landowners about your petition for a variance, the variance you seek, and the date and time of a hearing on the variance petition. With that information, those landowners will have the opportunity to attend the hearing and voice their comments. After the variance petition has progressed through that stage, hearings may follow before the planning commission and later before the governing body.

Going Before the Municipal Government

Before your community passes a new ordinance or a changed ordinance that will somehow affect your ability to keep and enjoy horses, the local government will announce the proposed change and hold one or more public hearings. If you plan to attend and speak out at a public hearing, keep these ideas in mind to improve your chances of success:

Remember your audience. Who runs the hearings and meetings of the planning commission or local governing body? Municipal leaders. These people have merely seen horses race at the track or patrol the downtown streets. Especially if you reside in the more urban areas, you can safely assume that these people have never owned horses. As a result, remember that you cannot appeal to them as horse lovers in order to win their support for your position.

Learn the lingo, and understand the legislative process in your community. Local government leaders speak a different language, or so it seems. Their talk is loaded with terms unfamiliar to most horse people. Learn them. Here are just a few of these terms:

- *Public hearing.* A public hearing is a proceeding open to the public where a municipal body evaluates possible action, such as enacting a new zoning regulation. Often, these hearings give members of the public (and their attorneys) a chance to comment on the proposed regulation or ask questions of the municipal leaders or consultants. Typically, under the law, the local government must hold a public hearing before amending a zoning ordinance.

- *Setback restriction.* Setback restrictions are restrictions that prevent a land owner from situating structures, such as barns or outbuildings, or fences within a certain distance from a property line, curb, or other structure.

- *Planning Commission or Planning Board.* State laws typically authorize local governments to establish zoning or planning commissions or boards. Generally speaking, these bodies are set up to advise the municipality on land restrictions and issues. In many cases, the planning commission will hold public hearings, take its own vote on a proposed zoning measure, and then submit a report to the municipal government. After that, the government can hold its own public hearings and then make its decision.

- *Grandfather clause.* A grandfather clause is a provision in a new law that exempts those who were not in compliance with the law when it took effect. For example, if a new zoning ordinance provides that horse barns must be located 50 feet or more from a lot line, a grandfather clause might provide that barns existing when the law took effect may continue their operations, even if the barns are located less than 50 feet from the lot line.

Keep aware of local government meeting agendas. Know where the local government publishes or posts meeting notices for its planning commission and governing body. Keep aware of whether the agenda includes matters of interest to you. Remember that the municipality must give advance notice of its agenda and cannot "sneak in" an important measure, such as a revamped horse ordinance, without following proper channels for advance notice and hearings to the residents.

Consider establishing an association. A well-organized group of horse proponents can strengthen the odds for success. The association can pool its resources and raise funds. Associations can also assign members to track important local government meeting dates, hire lawyers or consultants when needed, develop a network of interested members who will contact concerned residents about key meetings, evaluate zoning or land use ordinance proposals and developing reasonable alternatives, plan orderly presentations at public hearings, and share important information with concerned residents.

Consider exposing the community and its leadership to horses in a positive way. If you are allowed to do so, consider inviting local planning commissioners and community leaders to a friendly, well-organized "open house" or community barn tour. In planning the event, of course, you will hand-pick presentable facilities, invite all members of the planning commission, local government, and others, and tour the guests through the facilities. This type of event might help them abandon long-held prejudices that horses somehow generate foul sights, sounds, and odors, or that horses threaten property values.

Seek to gain the community's support through community activities. Another example of ways in which horse supporters can develop good community relations is to hold fund-raising activities with an equine theme. For example, a leader in the community where this author lives has organized the "Franklin, Michigan Fox Hunt." In this event, several riders from Southeast Michigan gather on horseback for a fun, quiet ride through the streets of Franklin (a quaint suburb of Detroit, Michigan) and in pastures of cooperative residents, with a gathering in the town square. An invitation-only dinner reception follows, which is well-attended by municipal leaders. All participants must make a cash donation to the community association. The event has been successful. In 1997, for example, it raised several thousand dollars, which were earmarked for the community association to install quaint, new street signs and plant new trees. Without question, the event strengthened ties between the horse supporters and the community.

What to Consider
When the Hearings and Proposals Begin

Let's assume that the municipality has drafted a proposed new ordinance, or it seeks to change the old one, that affects horse keeping. The process, which some might call a "battle," has begun. Now, more than ever, your need for organization is paramount. Here are some ideas:

Read all ordinance proposals very carefully. If the municipality presents a proposal to change an existing ordinance or to enact a new one, read it *very* carefully. Understand exactly how the proposed new ordinance varies from the old, and consider drafting a chart that thoroughly compares features of the two.

Plan a careful and reasonable strategy. Threatening the local government or its members is a sure promise of failure. Be reasonable when addressing the local planning commission or governing body. Be respectful, not disruptive, at meetings. Show the municipal leaders that you share their concerns.

Some business people, such as real estate developers who have had success with local governments, have been known to remain in attendance at municipal meetings long after the hearing on their issue has ended. Just a few hours of quiet attendance—in which they do nothing more than sit quietly near the front row while the meeting continues—can have tremendous impact on the decision makers and help earn their respect.

Consider appointing a "leader." A likeable member of the community, particularly someone who has earned respect in the community or has a distinguished history of serving in local government positions, will help lend credibility to your group when addressing the local government.

Listen to the municipal leaders. Where allowed by law (Open Meetings Act laws or similar laws require almost all local government meetings to take place in public), consider meeting with members of the municipal body before or between hearings on your issue, even if these people do not share your support of horses. Discuss their concerns. Talking to those on the other side of the proposal might be far more productive than you think.

Keep in mind that a strategy of confronting local officials can be risky, especially if you confront them before a scheduled vote. At this stage, it is possible that you will be perceived as trying to influence their vote. Many officials will avoid meeting with you to avoid even the appearance of influence, and your credibility could be impaired as a result.

Listen to the non-horse members of your community. What are the non-horse-oriented residents of your community saying about a proposed ordinance or change? Consider meeting with them. Explain your proposal and try to gain their support. Ask for their comments and listen carefully. Their comments might prompt you to alter or modify the zoning change you are proposing. By listening to their concerns and taking them into account, you will be ready to respond to objections at the public hearings—or you may have avoided objections entirely. You may also have expanded your list of supporters.

Borrow helpful language from other ordinances. Municipal governments frequently borrow language from other community ordinances. If you can locate favorable ordinances from nearby areas—especially ordinances that have been in effect, without challenge, for years—consider presenting them to your own municipality. You might be able to use their words as an alternative to an unfavorable proposal at issue.

Actively involve your allies. Because municipal leaders typically fear making unpopular decisions, there is strength in numbers. When important hearings or meetings take place, bring as many people as possible. Written petitions loaded with signatures are helpful, but a room full of concerned, cooperative constituents can say far more.

Accentuate the positive. Help the municipality's leaders understand the true importance of horses to the community. For example, discuss how the community's children are involved with horses and the degree of responsibility that horses foster. Explain how horses are central to community and school activities, such as Pony Clubs or 4-H programs, equestrian teams, handicapped riding programs, local horse shows, or other organized activities. Consider proving how horse shows and equine events have brought revenue into the community.

Understand the municipality's established procedures. Make sure that the municipality has not overstepped its bounds and has followed its established rules and procedures for meetings and hearings. For example, make sure that the municipal body has posted or published its meeting notices sufficiently in advance of a meeting.

Never underestimate the importance of professional help.
Zoning battles are not just neighborhood discussions. They involve legal issues. A lawyer, whether he or she works behind the scenes or as a visible member of the group, can help improve your chances of success. For example, a lawyer can address the municipality (where appropriate), retain professional planning consultants or environmental consultants, help select effective residents to address the municipality, review or write statements for residents to present at public hearings, develop effective relations with the media, and more.

When all else fails, sometimes zoning and land use conflicts must be resolved through the court system. A lawyer can evaluate whether an ordinance at issue, the manner in which it is applied, or the manner in which it was enacted is a proper target of a legal challenge.

What to Consider Before an Equine Professional Conducts Business in Your Barn

Ann, a widow, owns a horse stable. The stable was last used many years ago when her children owned and showed horses. Now, the children have grown and moved on, the barn is vacant, and cobwebs have overtaken the stalls. Paul, a horse trainer and riding instructor, has approached Ann with an offer: he will use her barn as the "home base" for his horse training and boarding operations. In exchange, he will pay Ann a monthly rent payment.

Sue trains Gene's horses in exchange for free room and board at his stable. Gene, a businessman who is usually out of town, also allows Sue to operate her own independent activities, such as riding lessons, on the premises. For years, Gene and Sue were perfectly happy with the arrangement, until the day when one of Sue's students got hurt during a lesson. When it happened, Gene was out of the country on a business trip. The student, however, has sued both Sue and Gene. Neither one had insurance.

Barn sharing or leasing arrangements can be riddled with risk, especially if you are the property owner. If you are considering this kind of arrangement, it helps to understand the risks and to answer these questions:

- How will the professional's planned use affect me?
- Will the professional have a reasonable chance to do business with minimal disruption?
- Have the parties planned in advance for, and adequately protected themselves against, possible liabilities that could arise from the use of the property?
- How does insurance affect the arrangement?
- Do zoning ordinances affect the professional's planned use?
- Can the arrangement be reduced to a written contract?

How Will the Professional's Planned Use Affect Me?

Virtually overnight, Ann's tranquil country setting could be transformed into a bustling equine business with a flurry of visitors, horses, cars, trucks, motor homes, and trailers. Is Ann ready for this?

Through a carefully worded contract (preferably drafted with the help of a knowledgeable lawyer), Ann might want to restrict Paul's use of the property within limits she can accept. For example, Ann might want to specify that Paul can have no more than 20 visitors at any given time. She could designate a certain area for trailer and car parking. She could forbid Paul or his visitors from entering her home or allowing their horses on her lawn. Also, knowing Paul's interest in holding occasional training clinics or shows on the land, their contract could demand that Paul receive Ann's advance written permission before these activities can take place.

Will the Professional Have a Reasonable Chance to Do Business With Minimal Disruption?

Paul may have bargained to do his business in Ann's barn, but did he expect that the arrangement would include baby-sitting Ann's grandchildren (who approach unruly horses and unlatch gates)?

With these concerns in mind, Paul would be wise to minimize the degree of interference in his operations. He can insist that Ann has the right to enter and inspect her barn, but her grandchildren cannot (unless Paul and Ann arrange visits for a mutually convenient time).

Have the Parties Planned in Advance For, and Adequately Protected Themselves Against, Possible Liabilities That Could Arise From the Use of the Property?

Liability is an issue of concern to everyone in a barn sharing or leasing arrangement. This means, for example, that even though Ann does not participate in Paul's business activities, she will likely be sued if someone gets hurt. The sad reality is, lawyers who represent injured people will usually try to sue persons or businesses having any possible connection to the horse, land, or business operations. Everyone joined in the suit will need to retain legal counsel, and they will try to remove themselves from the case. Whether these efforts win or lose, the cost of a legal defense can be tremendous.

Ann should make sure that Paul has adequately protected himself and her against liabilities that could result in a lawsuit against both of them. For example:

- *Equine Liability Laws.* Ann can make sure that Paul knows of an equine activity liability law in her state. As of January 2000, 44 states have passed these types of laws. In particular, Ann may want to make sure that Paul has complied with any warning sign posting requirements and that he is aware of any special provisions that may affect the language he uses in his contracts and releases. [Chapter Two addresses contract language requirements.]

- *Insurance.* When Gene allowed Sue to give riding lessons on his land, he never imagined that one day—when he was thousands of miles away—Sue's business activities could make him a target in a lawsuit. This type of sad reality makes it more important than ever for both the barn owner and equine professional to plan ahead with proper insurance. Sue can purchase a professional liability policy and/or commercial general liability policy designed to cover her business operations. Sue can discuss with her insurance agent adding Gene as an "additional named insured" on her policies. This way, if somebody should sue Gene and Sue, the insurance can protect both of them.

- *Liability Releases.* Where releases of liability (also called waivers) are allowed by law, both the equine professional and the property owner can require everyone of legal age entering the property to sign one. A carefully worded release of liability will have language designed to protect the professional, the land owners, and others.

How Does Insurance Affect the Arrangement?

Nowadays, facilities stabling horses have numerous types of insurance available to them. The differences are very important. Ann should discuss the arrangement with her insurance agent before she signs a contract or allows Paul on the land. Chances are good that her agent will advise her to make many changes in coverage, which could translate into a more expensive insurance premium.

Before Paul entered the picture, for example, Ann probably only had homeowner's or farm-owner's insurance, which was designed, in part, to address possible liabilities when her social guests, friends, or maybe even trespassers suffered injuries or damage on her property. With the arrangement Paul is proposing, and the fact that he will pay her a regular rent fee, homeowner's insurance will probably not be enough. (Basic homeowner's insurance policies contain exclusions that apply when the insured person or land is part of a "business pursuit.")

The fact is, when a business activity takes place, someone will need to buy business insurance. Who will do this—Ann or Paul? Who will pay for it? What policy limits will remain in effect? Who will be named as "additional insureds" on the policy? Ann and Paul will need to discuss these matters.

Do Zoning Ordinances Affect the Professional's Planned Use?

From the start, local laws and ordinances can kill plans for a barn use or lease arrangement. Evaluate them before the arrangement gets started.

For example, local zoning ordinances might prevent the barn-use arrangement altogether. Years ago, Ann's horse activities may have been lawful because they were purely a family hobby, not a business offered to the public. The possibility exists that Ann's property cannot be zoned for the type of business use that Paul plans. Or, in the situation with Gene and Sue, maybe the local zoning ordinances would allow Sue to train only Gene's horses, because she lives on his property, but would not allow her to take in outside customers and horses for training and lessons.

What About a Contract?

Whenever land is leased or shared, the property owner and the one using the land would be wise to reduce the arrangement to a written contract, for their own protection. Handshake deals, while common in the horse industry, are difficult and costly to enforce in a court of law. Also, state laws (called the "Statute of Frauds") may require that contracts pertaining to an interest in land must be written in order to be enforceable.

What elements can the barn use/lease contract include? Here are just a few:

- *Security deposit.* Should the "tenant" pay the landowner a security deposit? A security deposit is a sum of money that would give the landowner some financial security in the event that the tenant damages the property or vacates without paying rent. State laws may address security deposits and whether, for example, they must be placed in a separate escrow account at the bank for safekeeping.

- *Permitted uses .* What can the equine professional do, or not do? A well-written contract will plan ahead, take into account the interests of both parties, and reasonably accommodate everyone's goals. That is, Ann might want to restrict Paul's hours of operation in order to keep the place reasonably quiet in the evenings. Gene might want to keep Sue from containing or spreading manure near his home, in order to control odors that might offend his business guests. Contracts can require the professional to comply with all zoning and land-use ordinances, fire codes, and other laws.

- *Lease term and termination.* How will the landowner know when the tenant has overstayed his or her welcome? Will the barn-use contract last for a year? Will it continue on a monthly basis unless terminated on one-month's prior notice (called a "month-to-month" lease term)? The contract should specify its duration and whether the parties intend for it to be self-renewing. The contract can also address what actions can be taken (also called "remedies") if either party fails to honor certain important obligations in the contract.

- *Payments, including amount and frequency.* How much does Ann or Gene expect to receive as payment? When? What if payments are not made timely, or, even worse, are missed? The contract can specify the details.

- *Assigning the contract to someone else or "sub-leasing" the barn.* Chances are good that Ann and Gene agreed to share their land with Paul and Sue because they relied on the other's integrity and trustworthiness. They never banked on having a slew of unknown professionals working there, as well. With this in mind, the contract can address whether the tenant can assign or sub-lease it to someone else.

- *Property maintenance.* What if Paul or Sue backs a tractor through a wall? What if a horse from the trainer's operations breaks through the fencing? Who will pay the cost of making repairs to the electrical wiring if things go bad?

- *Insurance.* Just as explained earlier, the barn use/lease arrangement can impact the insurance needs of everyone involved. Why assume that someone has bought it? Why assume that the other party is keeping it in effect? Get it in writing.

- *Releases of liability.* The lessor (someone in Ann or Gene's situation) might, for example, require the one leasing the land to sign a release of liability, where allowed by law. As noted earlier, the use of the land might also warrant that everyone who enters the property sign a release of liability, where allowed by law. Who writes the release, who presents it, and who it protects are among the factors for the parties to address in their contract.

- *Indemnification.* What if Ann is sued because Paul forgot to close the pasture gate, and one of his horses got loose, ran into the road, and injured the driver of a car? Indemnification language, explained earlier, can address this.

- *Resolving Disputes.* Maybe Paul and Ann would like to resolve their differences– if differences ever arise—through arbitration or mediation. This could potentially save them a substantial amount over the traditional legal system. Contract language allowing these options should be drafted with care because, unfortunately, not every dispute is appropriate for these alternatives. Possibly, Ann might want to reserve the sole right to select whether a dispute can proceed through mediation, arbitration, or the court system.

- *Attorney Fees.* Under the prevailing rule in the United States, the loser in a legal dispute is not automatically obligated to pay the winner's legal fees. Consequently, if the parties want to control the issue of who will pay attorney fees, the contract needs to spell it out.

A written contract that anticipates and addresses possible problems in the barn use/lease arrangement can save years of frustration, expense, and litigation down the line.

CHAPTER SEVEN

EQUINE LIABILITIES — THE LATEST DEVELOPMENTS AND HOW TO AVOID LIABILITY

How Have The Equine Activity Liability Laws Been Faring In The Courts? A Review Of The Court Cases

States With Equine Activity Liability Laws

As of January 2000, 44 states have passed laws that are designed to, in some way, control certain liabilities when people are injured in equine activities. These laws are commonly known as "Equine Activity Liability Laws." These laws are not identical, though many have characteristics in common. A list of all 44 statutes, and their citations, is included in Appendix A.

In general, the equine activity liability laws were designed to serve a variety of purposes, including to:

- Encourage continued existence of equine-related activities, facilities, and programs

- Give the equine industry strong defenses when lawsuits arise

- Help the equine industry better foresee, and, when possible prevent, the settings that give rise to liability and lawsuits

- Give stables, equine professionals, and others possible grounds in which to seek dismissal of lawsuits, without a trial, rather than undergo expensive trial proceedings

- When possible, focus certain equine-related injury cases on the "inherent risks" of equine activities rather than on the injured plaintiff

- Encourage the equine industry to use waivers/releases

- Teach people before they participate in equine-related activities about inherent risks and immunities that may impair their chances of winning a lawsuit, should they get hurt while riding or near horses.

The equine activity liability laws are *not* "zero liability laws." As you read on, you will see that these laws have blocked certain cases from succeeding but they do not, and were not intended to, make all liability involving horses a thing of the past.

What People Sue For

While it is true that most of the equine activity liability laws state that an "equine activity sponsor," "equine professional," or possibly others can be sued if injury, death or damage does *not* result from an "inherent risk" (a term defined in many of the laws), most of the laws contain a list of exceptions. These exceptions typically state that a lawsuit can proceed if someone is "participating in an equine activity" but an equine "professional," "equine activity sponsor," or another person did any of the following:

- Provided faulty tack or equipment that somehow caused injury, death, or damage to the participant.

- Failed to determine the participant's ability to safely manage the horse based on the participant's actual abilities or statements about his or her abilities.

- Owned, leased, or had lawful use of land or facilities that had a dangerous latent condition but for which no conspicuous (noticeable) warning signs were posted.

- A few cases have focused in some way on whether an "inherent risk" of the equine activity prevents the lawsuit.

- Many of the equine activity liability laws have exceptions that allow liability for "gross negligence," "willful and wanton misconduct," or intentional wrongdoing.

- Exceptions in a small number of the laws appear to allow lawsuits for ordinary negligence. States with such language in their equine activity liability acts include, but are not necessarily limited to, Florida, Kentucky, Maine, Michigan, Nebraska, New Jersey, New Mexico, North Carolina, Utah, and Virginia. [*Equine Law & Horse Sense* explains negligence and the equine activity liability laws.]

Summary of Court Cases

A. The exception of "faulty tack or equipment"

- *Vilhauer v. Horsemens' Sports, Inc.*, 598 N.W.2d 525 (South Dakota 1999). See summary of the case on page 147.

- *Young v. Brandt*, 485 S.E.2d 519 (Georgia App. 1997). The plaintiff was hurt when she was thrown and kicked by a horse. Her lawsuit claimed that the defendants—a stable and an equine professional—negligently gave her a horse with hunter-jumper tack (as opposed to a dressage saddle), failed to use a longe line, and placed her "in a position of unknown danger." At trial, the plaintiff won $250,000, but the Georgia Court of Appeals took the money away, finding that the plaintiff had assumed the risk of injury and, as a result, had no case.

- *Riehl v. B & B Livery, Inc.*, 960 P.2d 134 (Colorado 1998), *reversing*, 944 P.2d 642 (Colorado App. 1997). See summary of the case on page 148.

- *Easterling v. English Riding Stables, Inc.*, 1994 U.S. Dist. LEXIS 3470; 1994 WL 10155 (E.D. Louisiana 1994). The plaintiff fell when the horse she rode during a riding lesson allegedly bolted. Around the time of the fall, a martingale broke. The lawsuit argued that these exceptions in the Louisiana law, and possibly others, might apply: (1) the "faulty tack or equipment" exception; (2) the providing a horse and "failing to make reasonable and prudent efforts to determine the ability of the participant to engage safely in the equine activity" exception. The court ruled that the case could proceed to trial on these exceptions.

- *Patrick v. Sferra*, 855 P.2d 320 (Washington App. 1993). See summary of this case on page 151.

- *Day v. Snowmass Stables, Inc.*, 810 F. Supp. 289 (D. Colorado 1993). During a horse-drawn wagon ride organized by the defendant stable, a neck yoke ring broke on one of the wagons. When the horses with the broken harness collided with the plaintiff's wagon, the plaintiff fell off, and later sued. The court refused to dismiss the case because the Colorado Equine Activity Liability Act appeared to allow liability if "equine professionals" "provided equipment or tack and knew or should have known that the equipment or tack was faulty to the extent that it did cause injury." The broken neck yoke ring may have fit within that exception.

B. The exception of "fails to make reasonable and prudent efforts to determine the participant's ability to safely manage the horse"

- *Hendricks v. JAFI, Inc.*, 1999 Mass. Super. LEXIS 44; 1999 WL 1336069 (Massachusetts 1/20/99). The plaintiff was thrown from a horse during a riding lesson and later sued the stable based on exceptions in the Massachusetts Equine Activity Liability Act that an "equine professional" "provided the equine and failed to make reasonable and prudent efforts to determine the ability of the participant to engage safely in the equine activity . . . .." The trial court found the case to be viable and seemed to place a "continuing duty" on professionals to assess the participant's ability to safely manage the horse, even as the ride went on over time.

- *Riehl v. B & B Livery, Inc.* 960 P.2d 134 (Colorado 1998), *reversing*, 944 P.2d 642 (Colorado App. 1997). See summary of this case on page 148.

- *Young v. Brandt,* 485 S.E.2d 519 (Georgia App. 1997). See summary of this case on page 144.

- *Muller v. English,* 472 S.E.2d 448 (Georgia App. 1996). The plaintiff, an experienced rider, was hurt when she was kicked by a defendant's horse during a fox hunt. Her lawsuit was based on three exceptions under Georgia's equine activity liability act: (1) the defendants "provided an animal and failed to make reasonable and prudent efforts ..."; (2) the fox hunt land had a "dangerous latent condition" for which no warning signs were posted; (3) the rider of the horse that kicked her and the hunt club acted "in willful and wanton disregard" for her safety. The Georgia Court of Appeals found that exception (1) did not apply because the plaintiff rode her own horse—not a horse "provided" by someone else. The court also said exception (2) did not apply because the horse that kicked her was not a "dangerous latent condition" of the land. Finally, the court held that the plaintiff had no case under exception (3), of "willful and wanton" misconduct; the court found ample proof that "horses kick," and that the plaintiff, an experienced fox hunter, had to know this. Case dismissed.

- *Cave v. Davey Crockett Stables*, No. 03A01-9504-CV-00131 (Tennessee App. 1995). The plaintiff, a 12 year-old girl, was riding in a trail ride at a summer camp when the horse she rode galloped into a tree. The case was brought under these exceptions in Tennessee's equine activity liability act: (1) "failure to make reasonable and prudent efforts to determine the ability of the participant to safely manage the equine"; (2) acting in "willful and wanton disregard" for her safety; and (3) intentionally caused injuries. In its defense to the case, the camp brought written testimony (known as "affidavits") of camp workers proving that the camp followed all requirements in Tennessee's equine liability act. The plaintiff could not challenge this evidence. As a result, the court tossed out the case. The court of appeals agreed with the dismissal.

- *Easterling v. English Riding Stables, Inc.*, 1994 U.S. Dist. LEXIS 3470; 1994 WL 10155 (E.D. Louisiana 1994). See summary of this case on page 145.

- *Patrick v. Sferra*, 855 P.2d 320 (Washington App. 1993). See summary of this case on page 151.

C. The exception of "dangerous latent condition of the land"

- *Nielson v. AT & T*, 1999 WL 548482 (South Dakota 7/28/99). Six weeks after South Dakota's equine liability act took effect, the plaintiff and her daughter rode their horses at a gallop along a riding pasture that was leased by the Ellsworth Air Force Base Riding Club. Suddenly, the plaintiff's daughter's horse tripped and fell over, which killed the daughter. A cable trench that was dug by defendant AT& T was blamed for causing the horse to trip. The mother sued AT& T, claiming that it failed to fill the trench and failed to warn riders of the trench. The trial court threw out the case, mainly because of the South Dakota equine liability act, but the South Dakota Supreme Court—the state's highest court—disagreed; it concluded that even though the law appeared to protect "equine activity sponsors, equine professionals, and any other *person*" from liability, this law was not intended to benefit AT&T, because AT&T was not involved in equine activities. As a result, the case was brought back to court.

- *Muller v. English,* 472 S.E.2d 448 (Georgia App. 1996). See summary of this case on page 146.

D. The exceptions involving "gross negligence," "willful and wanton misconduct," or intentional wrongdoing

- *Lessman v. Rhodes,* 1999 WL 1063268 (Illinois App. 11/23/99). At a horse show, the plaintiff was warming up his horse in an arena but broke his leg when another competitor's horse, a stallion, kicked him. He sued the horse show sponsors, the rider of the horse who kicked him, and the owner of the kicking horse. He claimed, among other things, that the show managers should have (1) checked the backgrounds of the horses at the show; (2) kept a close watch on horses' behavior at the show; (3) separated stallions from other horses; and (4) made "kicker" horses wear red tail ribbons. The trial court found that the Illinois equine activity liability act prevented the lawsuit, and dismissed the case. When this decision was appealed, a key issue was whether the show sponsor's acts were in "willful and wanton disregard" of the plaintiff's safety at the show. The Illinois Court of Appeals, finding no evidence of that kind of wrongdoing, agreed that dismissal of the case was the right thing.

- *Vilhauer v. Horsemens' Sports, Inc.,* 598 N.W.2d 525 (South Dakota 1999). While working at the Corn Palace Stampede, the plaintiff was hit in the face with a gate. He sued the event sponsor, land owners, and several others. Apparently aware that South Dakota's equine liability law might hurt his chances of success, he asked the court to declare that law unconstitutional; the court did. However, the South Dakota Supreme Court disagreed. It reasoned that because the law did not shut the door to *all* lawsuits, and the law appeared to give people the right to sue for things such as faulty equipment or the defendants' "willful and wanton disregard" for his safety, the law was valid. The lawsuit could continue.

- *Faul v. Trahan*, 718 So.2d 1081 (Louisiana App. 1998). A race horse "flipped" onto the plaintiff, an exercise rider, before his exercise ride started. He was hurt and sued the racing stable. After a trial, the stable won, in part because it was unaware that the horse was dangerous. In dismissing the case, the judge noted that liability under Louisiana's equine activity liability act "is limited to circumstances constituting willful or wanton disregard for the safety of the participant" and intentional injuries. The problem was, the plaintiff's case never argued this degree of wrongdoing. The plaintiff tried to get the Louisiana Court of Appeals to rule otherwise, to no avail; that court said the case should be dismissed, too. That court also found that Louisiana's equine activity liability act did not violate the state's constitution.

- *Riehl v. B & B Livery, Inc.*, 960 P.2d 134 (Colorado 1998), *reversing*, 944 P.2d 642 (Colorado App. 1997). The plaintiff signed a liability release before she fell from a horse rented from the defendant's stable. Her lawsuit was based on these exceptions in Colorado's equine activity liability act: (1) failure to properly determine the plaintiff's riding abilities; (2) faulty tack or equipment; (3) willful, wanton, or gross negligence. The case went all the way to the Colorado Supreme Court, which ruled that the stable's release of liability was powerful enough to prevent the plaintiff's lawsuit for claims (1) and (2), but the release could not stop the plaintiff's case under (3) because Colorado generally does not allow releases to prevent suits under theories of "willful, wanton, or gross negligence." Consequently, the case could proceed on (3) only.

- *Gaurtreau v. Washington*, 672 So.2d 262 (Louisiana App. 1996). While mounted on a horse and waiting to enter a horse show arena, the plaintiff was kicked by a horse ridden by the defendant, a fellow exhibitor. A lawsuit followed. The trial court held that Louisiana's equine activity liability act prevented liability, and the plaintiff lost. The plaintiff appealed, but lost again. The Louisiana Court of Appeals ruled: (1) the defendant, a fellow competitor, could benefit from the Louisiana law because the law protected *"any other person,"* and he fit that category; (2) there was not enough evidence that the defendant acted in "willful and wanton disregard" for the plaintiff's safety because the horse he rode had never kicked anyone before; (3) it did not matter that the defendant failed to post a warning sign, because those sign posting requirements applied only to equine activity "sponsors" or "professionals"—the defendant, a show competitor, was not in those categories; and (4) the plaintiff's injuries were caused by "inherent risks" and no exceptions in the law supported a lawsuit against the defendant.

- *Muller v. English*, 472 S.E.2d 448 (Georgia App. 1996). See summary of this case on page 146.

- *Cave v. Davey Crockett Stables* , No. 03A01-9504-CV-00131 (Tennessee App. 1995). See summary of this case on page 146.

- *Patrick v. Sferra*, 855 P.2d 320 (Washington App. 1993). See summary of this case on page 151.

E. An "inherent risk," assumption of risk, or similar theories in the law prevents liability

- *Amburgey v. Sauder*, 238 Mich. App. 228 (1999). The plaintiff was invited to watch a friend take a riding lesson at the defendant's stable. When the lesson ended, she helped the student /friend groom the horse. As she walked down a barn aisle, she was bitten by a horse that allegedly lunged its head from a stall. At issue was whether Michigan's equine activity liability act even applied in this setting; the plaintiff argued that she was *not* an "equine activity participant" for whom the law applies. The trial court disagreed, finding that she was a "participant" because the definition of a "participant" in the Michigan law included people "visiting, touring, or utilizing an equine facility." Because of this, and because the plaintiff's injuries resulted from an "inherent risk of an equine activity," the court supported dismissal.

- *Eastley v. Wood*, No. 99-SC-0226 (New Hampshire Dist. Ct. 8/6/99). The plaintiff, a horseshoer, was trying to shoe the defendant's horse when the horse backed away and collided with his truck. The plaintiff's auto insurance covered all but $250 of the damage, and he sued the defendant horse owner to collect that amount. It appears that the court ruled that New Hampshire's equine liability law prevented the suit because the damage to the truck occurred in connection with an "equine activity."

- *Cooperman v. David*, 23 F. Supp.2d 1315 (D.Wyoming 1998). During a trail ride in Wyoming, the plaintiff's saddle slipped, and she was hurt. The court threw out the case, ruling that the risk of a slipping saddle was an "inherent risk" under the Wyoming Recreation Safety Act (that state's version of an equine activity liability act) for which suit could not be brought.

- *Young v. Brandt*, 485 S.E.2d 519 (Georgia App. 1997). See summary of this case on page 144.

- *Gaurtreau v. Washington*, 672 So.2d 262 (Louisiana App. 1996). See summary of this case on page 148.

- *Halpern v. Wheeldon*, 890 P.2d 562 (Wyoming 1995). Shortly after mounting a horse at the defendant's public riding stable, the plaintiff was thrown. Invoking the Wyoming Recreation Safety Act, the stable got the case tossed out of court on the basis that getting thrown was an "inherent risk" in riding a horse. The case was appealed to the Wyoming Supreme Court—Wyoming's highest court—which went the other way and reinstated the case, finding that the law did not clearly tell whether the risk of falling shortly after mounting was an "inherent risk" in horseback riding, or whether the stable could have cut the risks.

F. Some other exception or language in the equine liability law allows liability

- *Bothell v. Two Point Acres*, 965 P.2d 47 (Arizona App. 1998). The plaintiff, a 10 year-old child, was not even mounted on or riding a horse; instead, she was hurt while leading the defendant's horse and letting it graze when the horse took off and the lead rope got caught on her hand. She sued under Arizona's equine liability act (which follows a different set of exceptions than other states). The court held that the Arizona law did not shield the defendant horse owner from liability, and may have existed to allow suits such as this, because the girl, while holding the horse's lead shank, may have "taken control of the horse" (terms used in that state's law). The case could proceed.

G. The equine activity liability act does not apply to the case

- *Carl v. Resnick*, No. 97-3627 (Illinois App. 3/31/99). While trail riding in the Cook County Forest Preserve, the plaintiff met the defendant, who was riding with a friend. As the riders stopped to chat, one of the horses kicked the plaintiff. The plaintiff sued the owner of the kicking horse, claiming that the Illinois equine activity liability act did not apply because the plaintiff was riding her own horse at the time (as opposed to a horse that was "provided" to her from someone else). The trial court threw out the case. However, the case went up on appeal, and was reinstated. The Illinois appeals court, agreeing with the plaintiff, found that the Illinois equine liability act did *not* apply, but the court ruled that another law in that state—the Illinois Animal Control Act—gave the plaintiff a basis to sue.

- *Keller v. Merrick*, 955 P.2d 876 (Wyoming 1998). The plaintiff's parents bought a horse from the defendant for their son to ride. The defendant stated that the horse was gentle and well-trained for an inexperienced rider. One day after the sale, while the son was riding, the horse ran off uncontrollably, injuring him. A lawsuit followed. The court dismissed the case, finding that the Wyoming Recreation Safety Act (that state's equine liability law) prevented the case. After that, the case was appealed to the Wyoming Court of Appeals, which agreed that the equine liability law claims should be dismissed, but the case could proceed under different legal theories that apply to horse sales.

- *Dilallo v. Riding Safely, Inc.*, 687 So.2d 353 (Florida App. 1997). A court of appeals in Florida held that Florida's equine activity liability act took effect *after* suit was filed and played no role in the case.

- *Patrick v. Sferra*, 855 P.2d 320 (Washington App. 1993). The defendants gave the plaintiff an ex-race horse as a gift. The plaintiff rode and stabled the horse at defendants' facility for a few weeks. One day, while the plaintiff rode the horse, it bolted and the plaintiff fell. (There is evidence that the horse may have bolted with the plaintiff in earlier rides.) The plaintiff's suit was based on many exceptions in Washington's equine activity liability act, such as (1) "providing the equine and failing to make reasonable and prudent efforts . . ."; (2) faulty tack or equipment; (3) "wanton and willful" misconduct. The court threw out the case, and the Washington Court of Appeals agreed; it ruled that Washington's equine liability act did not apply because the plaintiff was hurt while riding her own horse. By comparison, the law might allow liability if the defendants had "provided" a horse. The plaintiff could not even sue under basic sales law, either, because the horse was *given* to her, not sold.

H. A valid liability release warrants dismissal of the case

- *Street v. Darwin Ranch*, 1999 WL 1029490 (D. Wyoming 11/12/99). The plaintiff fell from a horse and was hurt while trail riding at a Wyoming dude ranch. He sued. Before the ride, however, he signed the ranch's liability release. The court threw out his lawsuit, finding that he had signed away his right to sue. The court even noted that the release could stop the plaintiff from suing the ranch under Wyoming's Recreation Safety Act, which regulated equestrian liabilities (the plaintiff tried to argue that the release could not block a right to sue for violation of a law on the books).

- *Riehl v. B & B Livery, Inc.*, 960 P.2d 134 (Colorado 1998), *reversing*, 944 P.2d 642 (Colorado App. 1997). See summary of this case on page 148.

PUTTING THE EQUINE ACTIVITY LIABILITY LAWS TO THE TEST

In the horse industry, people often ask:

Do the equine liability laws really work?

Will my insurance rates decrease?

Is the horse industry seeing fewer lawsuits now that these laws have emerged?

Since all but six states have passed some form of equine liability law (as of January 2000), and since these laws have emerged only in the past decade or so, the industry now watches and waits.

The fact is, none of the equine liability laws is a complete "zero liability law." The laws contain exceptions which, by their terms, allow injured persons or others on their behalf to sue under certain circumstances. The previous section detailed exceptions and actual court cases. We will recap the exceptions, then look at how they could apply to the type of situations we find ourselves in when doing our horse activities.

Most *but not all* the laws allow an "equine activity sponsor," "equine professional," or possibly others referenced in the laws to be sued if the complained-of injury was not caused by an inherent risk but they:

- Provided tack or equipment that they knew or should have known was faulty, and the fault caused harm to the one partaking in an equine activity

- Improperly matched a horse with a rider or failed to determine the equine activity participant's ability to safely manage the horse, based on representations of his or her abilities

- Owned, leaseed, or had lawful use of land or facilities that had a dangerous latent (non-obvious) condition but for which no noticeable warning signs were posted

Laws in some states allow liability where "gross negligence" or intentional wrongdoing was committed. Laws in a small number of states appear to allow suits to proceed under the legal standard of "negligence" (which essentially is the failure to use reasonable care), but if the complained-of injury did not result from an "inherent risk."

152

Putting the Laws to the Test

Let's put three scenarios to the test and answer the question, how would the equine liability laws apply?

> *Before assigning Nathan Novice a mount to ride, Ryan the Wrangler asks: "How often have you ridden before?" Nathan replies: "I've ridden for 8 years" (without mentioning that he really has ridden only once in each of those years). Ryan assigns Nathan to ride Bullet, a spirited horse typically assigned to highly experienced riders at Ryan's stable. Nathan falls off and sues the stable.*

Under many of the existing equine liability laws, Nathan has grounds to sue. The equine liability law in Florida, for example, provides that an "equine activity sponsor," "equine professional," or any other person could face liability if they:

> [P]rovided the equine and failed to make reasonable and prudent efforts to determine the ability of the participant to engage safely in the equine activity, or to determine the ability of the participant to safely manage the particular equine based on the participant's representation of his ability.

Nathan, relying on this language, may argue that Ryan did not sufficiently assess his riding skills before assigning Bullet. Had Ryan asked only one or two more questions, he could have learned that Bullet was inappropriate for Nathan.

> *Betty Boarding Stable Owner owns a stable that offers boarding services but does not offer horseback rides or lessons to the public. One day, Mickey, a boarder, brings his girlfriend there to ride his horse. Mickey's horse throws his girlfriend. She now sues Betty, claiming Betty is legally responsible.*

Betty would likely win this one. Unlike the Norman Novice situation, Betty did not provide the horse—Mickey did. Just because Betty happens to stable Mickey's horse is not enough to make Betty legally responsible when the horse acts up while under Mickey's control.

A different set of facts, however, could change Betty's legal position altogether. What if Mickey's girlfriend claims that an unsafe condition of Betty's land caused the problem? Washington's equine liability law, for example, has an exception that allows a suit to proceed if an "equine activity sponsor" or "equine professional" "owns, leases, rents, or otherwise is in lawful possession and control of the land . . . upon which the participant sustained injuries because of a dangerous latent condition which was known to or should have been known to the equine activity sponsor or the equine professional and for which warning signs have not been conspicuously posted."

At the close of business one night, Reba Riding Instructor's assistant advises her that the bridle on Bart, one of Reba's school horses, has a broken buckle, which will cause it to fall apart. A tired Reba yawns, "I'll fix it first thing in the morning." Morning arrives, but Reba forgot to make the repairs. The bridle comes apart while Samantha Student is riding Bart. Samantha loses control of Bart, falls, and sues.

Under the equine liability laws in most states, Samantha could likely proceed under the "faulty tack or equipment" exception. The night before Samantha Student was injured, Reba's assistant alerted Reba to the broken bridle, but Reba did not make the repairs. Samantha's lawsuit would claim that her injuries resulted from the horse reacting uncontrollably to the broken bridle.

Numerous equine liability laws include the "faulty tack or equipment" exception. Ohio's law, for example, allows liability where the "equine activity sponsor, equine activity participant, equine professional, veterinarian, farrier, or other person provides . . . faulty or defective equipment or tack and knows or should know that the equipment or tack is faulty or defective, and the fault or defect . . . proximately causes the harm involved."

Conclusion

As these examples show, the potential for liability is still with us. The examples also illustrate the importance of reading and understanding the equine liability laws where you reside or do business. In the Appendix of this book is a list of all states with equine liability laws (as of January 2000).

UNDERSTANDING AND AVOIDING
EQUIPMENT RELATED LIABILITIES

Did you know that leather is a legal issue? Bridles and reins, martingales and harnesses, English saddles, Western saddles— these are necessary assets in equine activities. You should also be aware that these items can generate liabilities.

What Makes "Leather a Legal Issue"?

In the equine industry, faulty equipment—regardless of whether the equipment is made of leather, steel, polyester, cotton, or wood— is sometimes blamed for causing accidents and injuries. Consequently, those who have brought lawsuits over the years have asserted that someone either provided faulty equipment or improperly failed to detect and fix foreseeable equipment defects. For example, a 1992 Illinois court decision involved a plaintiff who sued a community center after a cinch strap broke during a ride, causing a fall from the horse and injuries. The plaintiff blamed the mishap on an allegedly "worn, dry, and old" cinch strap.

Virtually anyone in the horse industry risks becoming the target of an equipment-related lawsuit. The risk is especially apparent for professionals, such as riding instructors and horse rental facilities, who provide horses and ponies equipped with saddles, bridles, or harnesses. Those who provide hay rides and carriage rides are also targets for these suits.

The Basis for Liability

A lawsuit for personal injuries arising from defective equipment might be predicated on the legal theory of negligence or under a provision of an applicable equine activity liability law, depending on the law of the applicable state.

Negligence. "Negligence" is essentially the failure to use the degree of care that a reasonably prudent and careful person would use under similar circumstances. Where faulty tack or equipment is at issue, lawsuits typically assert that the equipment provider was negligent for using equipment known to be defective. Some lawsuits, such as cases involving

155

saddles slipping, have claimed that the provider or responsible person negligently failed to adjust the equipment properly.

Equine activity liability law. At least 41 of the 44 existing equine activity liability laws (as of January 2000) address certain liabilities associated with faulty equipment. These states include Alabama, Arizona, Arkansas, Colorado, Delaware, Florida, Georgia, Hawaii, Idaho, Illinois, Indiana, Iowa, Kansas, Kentucky, Louisiana, Maine, Massachusetts, Michigan, Minnesota, Missouri, Mississippi, Montana, Nebraska, New Hampshire, New Jersey, New Mexico, North Carolina, North Dakota, Ohio, Oklahoma, Oregon, Rhode Island, South Carolina, South Dakota, Tennessee, Texas, Utah, Virginia, Washington, West Virginia, and Wisconsin.

As one example of these equine liability laws, New Mexico's law reads, in part:

> Nothing in the Equine Liability Act shall be construed to prevent or limit the liability of the operator, owner, trainer, or promoter of an equine activity who ... provided the equipment or tack, and knew or should have known that the equipment or tack was faulty and an injury was the proximate result of the faulty condition of the tack.

What Defenses Are Available?

Defenses against equipment-related lawsuits can include, *but are not limited to*:

- The equipment had no defects, or the one being sued had no knowledge of any defects
- Even if the equipment were defective, the complained-of injuries did not result from (or "were not proximately caused by") the alleged defects
- The plaintiff's own negligence contributed to or caused his or her injuries (maybe the plaintiff herself improperly adjusted or altered the equipment)
- Assumption of risk (that is, the plaintiff may have known of a problem but proceeded anyway)
- A valid, legally enforceable written release or waiver of liability prevents the lawsuit

The effectiveness of these and other defenses will depend on the facts and applicable law. Sometimes, the tack or equipment manufacturer is blamed for the problem, and the lawsuit can become one of "products liability." The law of products liability is discussed elsewhere in this book.

Suggestions for Avoiding
Equipment Related Liabilities

Recognizing that unsafe equipment is an almost certain basis for a lawsuit, everyone in the horse industry can plan ahead to avoid liability. Here are some practical suggestions:

Equipment maintenance checks. If you provide horses to others—regardless of whether you are engaged in a horse-related business activity—try to inspect the equipment regularly. When doing this, look for cracks in the leather or worn-out areas from which cracks might develop. Check the condition of buckles and the leather around them. Look for rotted stitching. In saddles and bridles, areas especially prone to trouble are cheek pieces, stirrup leathers, cinches or girths, and billet straps (the leather straps that attach the girth or cinch to the saddle). If you provide Western saddles and bridles, keep a special watch on "Chicago screws." (These metal screws often secure the reins and bit to the bridle and usually can be tightened with a thin coin or screwdriver. To prevent the screws from loosening and breaking apart, some people suggest placing a few drops of nail polish inside the screws before tightening them.)

Equipment cleaning. Leather care products can effectively clean and prolong the life of horse-related equipment. However, when used improperly they can do more harm than good. With this in mind, make sure to read carefully the manufacturer's instructions. Keep in mind that some areas of saddles, such as billet straps, may not be suitable for oiling but can be treated with other products.

Repairs. The average horse owner or facility does not have special equipment, such as heavy-duty stitching machines and riveting devices, which are sometimes needed to repair tack and equipment. Consider hiring a reputable repair service, or replacing the broken equipment altogether, rather than risking a defective home remedy.

EIGHT STRATEGIES FOR AVOIDING LIABILITY

We all fear liability and rightly so. Liability can mean law-suits, trials, unpredictable jury verdicts, and the potential for serious financial liability. Everybody has the ability to take active measures in a continuing effort to avoid liability, and they should do so.

Here are eight strategies for avoiding liability.

1. Understand What Causes Liability

Everyone, it seems, offers opinions on liability in the horse industry. Many people, for example, call the equine liability laws "*zero liability laws.*" Some say that these laws have permanently ended all liability in the horse industry, but as you will see as you read this book, those statements are pure fiction. They originate from people who have never even seen the law. People who rely on these opinions could learn the hard way that they have been seriously misinformed.

Why allow unfounded opinions to steer you wrong on something as important as liability? In a continuing effort to avoid liability, it helps to separate fact from fiction. In this connection, learn about liability through books, articles, and seminars, and consult with a knowledgeable attorney when questions arise.

2. Develop Your Own Personal Safety Program

Be proactive by developing a personal safety program. Without question, a constant dedication to safety will reduce the risk of injuries and, consequently, liability. Through a series of safety-conscious habits and practices—implemented routinely—you *can* lessen the risk of liability. A safety program can include numerous things, but here are two ideas to help get you started:

Conduct regular equipment inspections. If you provide tack or equipment to others, chances are good that you are at risk for liability if the equipment is blamed for causing an injury, and the injured person claims that you knew or should have known about defects in the equipment. As explained earlier, many of the equine liability laws now impose liability under these circumstances. Knowing this risk is a good incentive to stay a step ahead. Regular equipment inspections will help keep your equipment in good condition and avoid liability on this basis.

Train your workers well. As a general rule, a business is liable for the negligent acts its employees commit in the course of their employment. With this in mind, your own dedication to safety is a good start, but make sure that your workers share it, too.

3. Don't Be Afraid to Use Liability Releases/Waivers

Contrary to popular belief, most states across the country have enforced releases of liability (also called "waivers") *if* they are properly worded, presented and signed. The next chapter discusses these documents.

When attempting to control liability, consider using carefully worded releases of liability. Form contracts found in books and sold in stores are, at best, a starting point. There is no substitute for a document that has been drafted by a knowledgeable attorney. And, of course, remember that having a waiver/release is never a substitute for having good insurance.

4. Good Insurance

Certainly, insurance will not prevent liability, although insurance can help save your home, your savings, and your property in the event that a claim or a lawsuit is brought against you. At the very least, insurance could spare you the enormous cost of a legal defense, if you are sued.

5. Read Your Equine Activity Liability Law Carefully

Because 44 states across the country have passed equine activity liability laws (as of January 2000), chances are good that an equine activity liability law exists in your state or in states where you do business. Read your law very carefully. Pay special attention to the law's exceptions.

6. Comply With Equine Activity Liability Law Sign-Posting Requirements

If an equine activity liability law affects you or your business, look for sign- posting requirements, and make sure that you comply. These requirements vary considerably from state to state; there is simply no "one-size-fits-all" sign for nationwide use. To illustrate how these requirements vary, Indiana's law requires warning signs to state:

> ### WARNING
>
> Under Indiana law, an equine professional is not liable for an injury to, or the death of, a participant in equine activities resulting from the inherent risks of the equine activities.

The Texas law, in comparison, requires citation of the state's equine activity liability law:

> ### WARNING
>
> UNDER TEXAS LAW (CHAPTER 87, CIVIL PRACTICE AND REMEDIES CODE), AN EQUINE PROFESSIONAL IS NOT LIABLE FOR AN INJURY TO OR THE DEATH OF A PARTICIPANT IN EQUINE ACTIVITIES RESULTING FROM THE INHERENT RISKS OF EQUINE ACTIVITIES.

Appendix A of this book lists the state equine liability laws that have sign posting requirements.

7. Comply With Equine Liability Law Contract Language Requirements That Affect You

Many of the equine liability laws also require that certain language (often, *but not always*, the same language required for warning signs) be repeated in various contracts. Equine professionals are usually targeted for this requirement. Chapter Two addresses these requirements.

8. Consider Establishing a Corporation or LLC

Establishing and maintaining a corporation or Limited Liability Company (LLC), just like having insurance, will not prevent liability. The entity could, however, spare your home, savings, and property if a lawsuit is brought against you. These entities are explained in Chapter Five of this book.

CHAPTER EIGHT

LIABILITY WAIVERS
AND RELEASES

Do You Need A Liability Release?

Joe operates a riding and boarding stable. His state has enforced liability releases in the past, but he has never used them. Instead, he posts one sign on his barn that says, "Ride at Your Own Risk." He believes the sign operates the same as a liability waiver or release and will completely prevent him from being sued if someone is hurt.

Jill boards a horse at Joe's stable. Before she left town for a vacation, Jill gave her friend permission to ride and handle her horse while she was away. Knowing that Joe's barn has posted a "Ride at Your Own Risk" sign, Jill believes that she does not need anything further to protect her from liability in case something should happen to her friend.

Are Joe and Jill correct? Does the posting of a sign make it unnecessary for them to use liability releases? Generally speaking, the answer is "No."

Warning signs are important and are, in fact, required under many state equine activity liability laws. But a sign is *not* the same as a release of liability (also called a "waiver"). This section explores the benefits of using both.

The Difference Between a Sign and a Release

There are important differences between posting a sign and using a release of liability that is legally valid, well written, and properly signed. Certainly, a sign that says "ride at your own risk" announces, in plain language, the facility's policy and intention of limiting its liability. When an incident arises, however, the injured person is almost certain to deny ever seeing the sign. Further, if an incident should occur while the customer or guest is not riding, such as a bite or kick, then the injured person will likely claim that the sign only applied to riding. Whether or not these arguments by the injured person have any merit is not the issue. What matters is that the mere posting of a sign is usually not enough to fend off a lawsuit when something goes wrong.

A release of liability, by comparison, can serve as an indication *in writing* that the visitor or customer has read, understood, and agreed to accept the facility's policy of limiting its liability. Also, as discussed here, the release provides an excellent opportunity to educate people about risks and more.

The Difference Between an Equine Activity Liability Law and a Release

If you live or do business in one of the 44 states with an equine activity liability law on the books (as of January 2000), you may have strong protection against many types of liabilities arising from certain equine activities. However, the laws were not designed to permanently end all liability in the horse industry. Because no "zero liability" laws exist, a written release of liability, where allowed by law, is an extra attempt to avoid liability.

Most states *do* enforce properly worded, presented, and signed releases. Even two states with equine activity liability laws have enforced written releases:

- In 1998, Colorado's highest court ruled that a liability release remained valid even after the enactment of the Colorado Equine Activity Liability Act. As a result, the court held, the release could waive liability *even* for claims that were based on the law's exceptions. Because established law in Colorado prevented releases from waiving liability for willful and wanton misconduct, however, the court allowed the lawsuit to proceed only on those claims. [The case was *Riehl v. B & B Livery, Inc.*, 960 P.2d 134 (Colorado 1998), discussed in the previous chapter.]

- In late 1999, the plaintiff argued that a dude ranch's liability release could not block his right to sue for violation of the Wyoming Recreation Safety Act (Wyoming's equine liability law). A federal court disagreed, enforced the release, and dismissed the case. [The case was *Street v. Darwin Ranch*, 1999 WL 1029490 (D. Wyoming 11/12/99), also discussed in the previous chapter.]

Extra Benefits of a Release of Liability

Posting a warning sign, especially where required by law, can be important, but a properly-worded release of liability has the potential to do much more. For example:

Recite risks. Most of the 44 equine activity liability laws acknowledge that certain equine activities involve "inherent risks" and state that "equine professionals, equine activity sponsors," and possibly others cannot be sued if a participant is injured or dies as a result of an "inherent risk of an equine activity" (subject to the law's exceptions). A release of liability can recite the inherent risks and other risks. This information about risks can be especially informative if the release is given to those with little experience around horses.

Headgear warning. The release can advise visitors, customers, or guests about wearing ASTM-standard/SEI-certified equestrian helmets. (Currently, protective headgear meeting these standards is proven to be most effective.)

Require health insurance. A small number of equine facilities require all customers or guests to maintain their own medical insurance as a condition of entering the premises. Some of these facilities require customers to identify their health insurance carrier and policy number. For these facilities, the release can make this requirement and information part of a binding contract, not just a policy.

Affirm its binding effect. If Jill's friend should become injured while taking a trail ride off the stable's property, he or she might assert that the "Ride at Your Own Risk" policy posted on the barn does not apply. Whether or not this argument is valid, a release can seek to stop this claim by specifying that the release is binding when the visitor or guest rides or is near horses *at any location*.

Include equine activity liability act notices. Most states with equine activity liability laws require certain persons—usually, but not always, equine professionals—to include warning notices or other language in their contracts and releases. In a small number of states, the equine liability laws indicate that those who fail to follow these requirements could lose the benefit of any immunities in their laws. Chapter Two addresses these requirements.

Spare the need to post warning signs. In Florida, for example, the equine activity liability act states that "equine professionals" or "equine activity sponsors" are spared the burden of posting warning signs if they use written contracts that include the same "warning" language. This could relieve some riding instructors, who may give lessons at several different places in the same day, of the need to bring along and post their own written "warning" signs.

WHY LIABILITY RELEASES FAIL—AND HOW YOU CAN IMPROVE YOUR CHANCES OF SUCCESS

"Liability releases are not worth the paper they're written on." We hear statements like this all the time. Are they true?

Generally speaking, no. What *is* true, however, is that releases of liability (also called "waivers") are probably the most misunderstood documents in the horse industry. In fact, most states *will* enforce releases of liability, This fact surprises many in the horse industry because we most commonly hear of releases failing.

There are three main reasons why liability releases fail:

1. A state's law makes releases invalid

2. The release had defective language

3. There was a serious problem or defect in the manner in which the release was presented or signed

This section addresses each of them. Also, if you seek to reduce your liability by using releases, this section explains how to improve your chances for making your document *succeed* through effective language, proper presentation, and knowing when to discard it.

Failure Reason 1:
A State's Law Makes Releases Invalid

A *very* small number of states have laws on the books that invalidate releases used in equine, sporting, or recreational activities. Some of the laws appear to prevent equine professionals from relying on releases to avoid liability in their activities.

Even within states having a history of enforcing releases, courts frequently (but not always) recognize that people cannot release (give away) the right to sue for certain types of serious wrongdoing, such as:

- "Gross negligence"
- "Willful and wanton misconduct" or
- Intentional misconduct

Failure Reason 2:
The Release Had Defective Language

Ineffective language found in the document itself is the most common reason a release of liability fails. You may not spot the deficiencies, but a judge and a trained lawyer will. When a liability release is subjected to a legal challenge, it is guaranteed to receive *very* intense scrutiny, as if it were placed under a microscope. Every word in the document will be examined closely.

The problem of defective wording usually is not discovered until a lawsuit puts the release to the test. In a 1993 lawsuit against an equestrian center in Ohio, for example, the Court struck down the document, finding faulty language. The document was termed a "release" but failed to carefully specify that the signer was releasing the center from liability for its own negligence or legal liability. Instead, the "release" document released the center from liability arising from the consequences of *the signer's* negligence. [The case was: *Tanker v. North Crest Equestrian Center*, 621 N.E.2d 589 (Ohio App. 1993).]

As examples of some releases that have worked, here are portions of releases of liability that were *upheld* and found to be valid by courts in Colorado, Indiana, California, and Massachusetts.

Colorado Example

The Colorado Supreme Court, in a 1999 decision, upheld the release below that stated, in part:

> I, _____ understand the potential dangers that I could incur in mounting a horse and in riding on said horse. Understanding those risks I do hereby advise and represent and warrant to B & B Livery, Inc., that I do hereby release that Company, its officers, directors, shareholders, employees and anyone else directly or indirectly connected with that Company from any liability in the event of any injury or damage of any nature (or perhaps even death) to me or anyone else caused by my electing to mount and then ride a horse owned or operated by B&B Livery, Inc.
>
> This release shall be binding not only upon me but also upon my heirs, my personal representatives and legal representatives and anyone who could claim an interest through me. I have executed this release willingly and after having read or been advised of the warning posted by B&B Livery, Inc., which warning states as follows: Under Colorado Law, an equine professional is not liable for an injury to or the death of a participant in equine activities resulting from the inherent risks of equine activities pursuant to section 13-21-119 Colorado Revised Statutes.

167

Indiana Example

In a 1997 case, an Indiana court enforced a release that stated, in part:

> I hereby acknowledge that I have voluntarily applied to participate in an activity of horseback riding with Turkey Run Saddle Barn.
>
> I understand that the activity of horseback riding involves numerous risks of injury that are my responsibility, and I assume these risks. I further understand that an animal, irrespective of its training and usual past behavior and characteristics, may act or react unpredictable at times based upon instinct or fright which is a risk to be assumed by each participant in the riding activity.
>
> To participate in the activity of horseback riding, I hereby release from any legal liability Turkey Run Saddle Barn and any employees for any injury or death caused by or resulting from my participation in the activity of horseback riding. I agree not to sue, claim against, attach the property of or prosecute the Turkey Run Saddle Barn or any employee.
>
> This contract shall be legally binding on me . . .
>
> I have carefully read this agreement and fully agree with its contents.

California Example

A California court upheld the following liability release, which was printed in capital letters throughout.

> RELEASE
>
> I HEREBY RELEASE [THE ACADEMY], CHARLES KOOPMAN, DONNA KOOPMAN, MANAGERS, TRAINERS, INSTRUCTORS AND EMPLOYEES OF AND FROM ALL CLAIMS WHICH MAY HERE-AFTER DEVELOP OR ACCRUE TO ME ON ACCOUNT OF, OR BY REASON OF, ANY INJURY, LOSS, OR DAMAGE, WHICH MAY BE SUFFERED BY ME OR TO ANY PROPERTY, BECAUSE OF ANY MATTER, THING OR CONDITION, NEGLIGENCE OR DEFAULT WHATSOEVER, AND I HEREBY ASSUME AND ACCEPT THE FULL RISK AND DANGER OF ANY HURT, INJURY OR DAMAGE WHICH MAY OCCUR THROUGH OR BY REASON OF ANY MATTER, THING OR CONDITION, NEGLIGENCE OR DEFAULT, OF ANY PERSON OR PERSONS WHATSOEVER.

Massachusetts Example

Finally, below is part of a liability release that a Massachusetts court recently found powerful enough to dismiss a lawsuit against a stable.

RELEASE FORM

PLEASE READ THIS DOCUMENT CAREFULLY AND DO NOT SIGN IT UNLESS YOU FULLY UNDERSTAND IT.

Student's Name: _____

I recognize the inherent risks of injury involved in horseback riding generally and in learning to ride in particular. In taking lessons at Woodlock Farm, I assume any such risk of injury and further, I voluntarily release Woodlock Farm, its instructors, and agents from any responsibility on account of any injury I or my child or ward may sustain while receiving instruction or while riding in connection therewith, and I agree to indemnify and hold harmless Woodlock Farm, its instructors, and agents on account of any such claim ...

WARNING

Under Massachusetts Law, an equine professional is not liable for an injury to, or the death of, a participant in equine activities resulting from the inherent risks of equine activities, pursuant to Chapter 128, Section 2D of the General Laws.

Student's Name: _____ Date: _____

Because intense scrutiny is virtually assured where a liability release is involved, do not take chances with your documents. Make sure that they comply with the legal requirements of your state.

Failure Reason 3:
There Was a Serious Problem or Defect in the Manner in Which the Release Was Presented or Signed

Good wording in a liability release is only the first step; even the best worded liability release runs a risk of failure if there was some legally significant defect in the manner in which it was presented and signed. Here are some examples of how releases have failed based on claims that they were presented improperly:

- The signer of the release claims to have been under the influence of alcohol or drugs at the time he or she signed it

- Minors (children typically under the age of 18) certainly can sign releases, but they are usually permitted by law to disaffirm the agreement later on

- With minors, the signature of a trainer, uncle, or family friend will not suffice, unless that person is a parent or legal guardian who is expressly signing the release on behalf of a child. The law of releases as applied to children is *very* complex, and not always can the minor child's parent or legal guardian release away the child's right to sue.

How You Can Improve Your Chances for Success Through Effective Language in the Release

Individuals, professionals, and businesses in the equine industry can consider many elements for their releases of liability. [These elements are more fully explained in *Equine Law & Horse Sense*.] Here are some of them:

- Make sure that the release is written in clear, straightforward language
- Let the document's own title reaffirm that it is a waiver or release of liability
- State the signer's name, address, and phone number and whether he or she is signing as a minor's parent or legally-appointed guardian. Include the minor child's name and age
- Mention certain inherent risks and consider listing examples, but note that you are only providing *some* examples
- Pay special attention to whether the "exculpatory language" in the release (the part in which the signer, on his or her own behalf and/or on behalf of a child, agrees not to sue) complies with any requirements under the applicable state's law
- Pay attention to contract language requirements that might be imposed by an equine activity liability law. These requirements are addressed in Chapter Two of this book

These are just some elements in releases that can help make a difference.

How to Improve the Chances for Success by Properly Presenting the Release

Sometimes, how you present a release of liability and ask others to sign it can be just as important as the language contained in the document. Here are some tips for presenting a release:

- Give the signer a reasonable opportunity to read it
- Do not cover up parts of a release before asking someone to sign it
- If the signer tells you that he or she is dyslexic or cannot read English, offer to read the release to that person. Make your

records clearly reflect that this was done, by whom, when, and at whose request. In a 1993 lawsuit, a court rejected the signer's argument that the release was invalid because he could not read English when he signed it. In that case, the release clearly stated above his signature: "I Have Read this Release." The court held that the *signer* had the duty to speak up about his inability to read, and he could have asked to have the release read or explained to him. Because he failed to do any of these things, the release was enforced and his case tossed out.

How Long Does a Signed Release "Last"?

Should you make someone re-sign the same release document each time he or she enters your property, rides your horses, or even comes near your horses? Of the many factors that may affect the answer, here are two:

First, how is the release worded? If the release, for example, states that it is effective *today* only, you will need a newly signed document tomorrow. Or, if the release, by its terms, applies strictly to horseback riding but the guest or visitor is now doing something else, it may be time to present a new release document with different language.

Second, how does the applicable state's law address the situation? For example, Ohio's law makes waivers used in college or university equine activities valid for 12 months.

Know When to Part With the Release

After your release comes back from someone else, completely signed, how long must you keep it? If you are the one the release protects, it helps to keep the document until you are *absolutely* positive that the applicable statute of limitations for a lawsuit has expired. When in doubt, file the release in a secure place as long as possible, and do not destroy it until after you have received reliable advice, preferably from a knowledgeable attorney.

Stay Adequately Insured

Having a release does not eliminate the need for proper insurance. Insurance is designed to pay for your legal defense and (up to policy limits) settle a claim or pay any damages that you may be legally ordered to pay if you are sued by someone who has signed your release. Unfortunately, even if your state has enforced releases in the past, there is never an absolute guarantee that all courts will accept and enforce your release.

CHAPTER NINE

OTHER LEGAL RIGHTS YOU SHOULD KNOW

Looks Like Veterinary Malpractice—
Now What?

Your dreams shatter before your eyes. Your yearling—the one with impeccable breeding, perfect conformation, and the one around whom you had planned your future in the horse business—is about to be put down. Veterinary specialists at the university told you that nothing in modern medicine could be done to save him. They explained that the damage might have been prevented with a better or quicker diagnosis or with more timely intervention by your veterinarian. Your veterinarian, it seems, had mis-diagnosed and mistreated the very problem that will now end your horse's life. You want to make the veterinarian pay for his apparent mistakes—for the loss of your horse and the loss of the future the horse promised you. You want to sue your vet for malpractice. Do you have a case? And if you do, can you find a lawyer who is willing to handle it for you?

Just because you have a veterinary malpractice case that might win does not mean that you can find a lawyer to take it. Worse yet, you may be surprised to learn that your victory may yield little compensation for your losses.

This section explores:

- How the law defines veterinary malpractice
- What it takes to prove a winning case for veterinary malpractice
- If you win your case, how much money you can receive
- How to develop facts to support your case
- When you must file your suit
- Why it is often harder to find a lawyer than to prove your case
- Other ways to fight if you believe your veterinarian has erred

What is Veterinary Malpractice?

Generally speaking, the law imposes on veterinarians a duty to use reasonable skill, diligence and attention, as may ordinarily be expected

175

of a careful and skillful person in the same profession. If a veterinarian falls short of this standard when treating your horse, you may have grounds to support a legal action against him or her for veterinary malpractice.

Over the years, veterinary malpractice actions have been brought for mis-diagnosing a horse's maladies, administering improper medications or improper dosages, improperly performing surgery, improper follow-up care, and many others. Veterinary malpractice lawsuits are filed with far less frequency than medical malpractice lawsuits. The reason is simple: the law looks at animals, and their values, in a different way than we, as animal enthusiasts, do. As a result, in most states, you stand to win far less if the case involves veterinary malpractice than you would if the matter involves an injured human.

Proving Veterinary Malpractice

Proving veterinary malpractice is not always easy. A veterinarian will rarely admit that he or she has erred. Rather, the law demands that the aggrieved party (the plaintiff) must identify and specifically prove how the veterinarian erred. Successful cases typically require the plaintiff to prove the following:

- First, the veterinarian had a legally recognized duty to handle a professional matter in a certain way.

- Second, the veterinarian somehow departed from, or "breached," that duty. Over the last several years it has become more important than ever to prove this through the testimony of a knowledgeable expert witness.

- Third, a plaintiff must prove "proximate cause." This essentially means that the one bringing a veterinary malpractice case must prove that the veterinarian's malfeasance (wrongful conduct), and not some other reason, caused the horse's demise or devaluation.

- Finally, a plaintiff must prove with reasonable certainty a sum of money or value that has been lost as a result of the malpractice (called "damages"). In animal-related cases, proving damages can sometimes be the biggest problem of all.

Why the Need for Expert Testimony?

Expert testimony in malpractice cases can be very important. In fact, courts in many states have held that expert witness testimony is *required* in order to win in a veterinary malpractice case. The right expert witness is typically another veterinarian who knows the standard of care that your veterinarian should have followed.

Merely having *an expert* is not the same as having *the right expert*. Be prepared for the court to evaluate your expert's credentials and opinion. In some cases, the court can even refuse to let your expert testify if the expert lacks sufficient qualifications or provides opinions that are not reliable or not based on legitimate scientific information.

What Damages Can the Winning Plaintiff Collect?

Damages in veterinary malpractice actions can include any of the following:

- If the horse has died, its fair market value around the time of death
- If the horse survives the alleged malpractice, the amount of money in which the horse has decreased in value
- Lost profits such as stud fees or offspring
- The likely value of lost race or show profits
- The value of time spent caring for the injured animal
- Money spent in caring for the horse after the wrongdoing
- The cost of procuring a substitute horse for the interests or purposes served by the horse who, you believe, was victimized by malpractice

Other types of damages, which are very rarely awarded in veterinary malpractice cases, include money to compensate for the animal owner's pain and suffering, punitive damages, and attorney fees. It usually takes extreme wrongdoing for a court to even consider awarding the recovery of these types of damages. A knowledgeable lawyer can determine what damages the state at issue will grant to winning parties in veterinary malpractice cases.

States vary on what the winning plaintiff in a veterinary malpractice case may collect. In 1996, a Florida jury verdict awarded $950,000 to the owner of an accomplished race horse. In 1998, a California jury returned a verdict of $600,000 against two veterinarians alleged to have wrongly injected a race horse. These were among the largest jury verdicts ever issued in veterinary malpractice cases.

Going back to the example at the beginning, how could you prove the value of a yearling that has not yet been proven through his performance on the track, in the show ring, or as a breeding animal? This is a serious problem, but one you might overcome. For example, you might hire as an expert witness an equine appraiser or an independent person knowledgeable of the industry and the horse's chance for success. This type of testimony might make a difference in a veterinary malpractice lawsuit.

How Can You Develop Information to Support a Case?

A lawsuit is only as good as the evidence the plaintiff can present. Sometimes, a horse owner discovers the idea of bringing a veterinary malpractice case long after the horse has already been destroyed. By that time, the owner may have lost the opportunity to have the animal examined independently or through a post-mortem examination.

With this in mind, if you suspect veterinary malpractice, secure as much evidence as possible of the horse's condition and the wrongdoing you believe the veterinarian committed. If it would be humane to do so, consider obtaining a second opinion, including X-rays, blood work, and tissue samples, by a respected veterinarian or facility. If the horse must be destroyed, consider ordering an immediate necropsy (autopsy) by a qualified professional, along with a carefully written report, or see if the carcass can be preserved for later evaluation.

When Must Suit be Brought?

Don't wait if you suspect malpractice. Almost every state has a law that specifically limits the time in which licensed professionals, such as veterinarians, can be sued for malpractice. These laws are known as "statutes of limitations" and they vary from state to state. In Michigan, for instance, the statute of limitations for a veterinary malpractice lawsuit is only two years from the date of the last treatment or six months from the date the malpractice was discovered, whichever occurs last.

In some instances, the lawsuit against the veterinarian will involve basic negligence or carelessness—not necessarily veterinary malpractice. For example, the veterinarian's staff might have placed the horse in a negligently designed horse stall, which caused the horse to be injured at the clinic. In this situation, the legal matter might have nothing to do with veterinary malpractice. Because of this, the applicable state law might allow a different, usually longer, statute of limitations for which to bring suit.

Finding a Lawyer to Handle Your Case

Even if you have a strong veterinary malpractice case, finding a lawyer to handle it for you can be a tremendous problem. Why? In the vast majority of states, the winning plaintiff in a veterinary malpractice case stands to recover far less than what he or she would have recovered if the matter involved human medical malpractice. The limited amount of damages the winning plaintiff can usually recover in veterinary malpractice cases, the potential for time-consuming litigation, and the high cost of hiring expert witnesses to substantiate the malpractice and the damages make lawyers reluctant to handle these cases under a contingency fee arrangement—unless the evidence is very strong and the damages at stake truly warrant this arrangement.

Other Options and Alternatives to the Malpractice Case

You have options in addition, or as an alternative, to a malpractice case. Here are two:

Challenge the veterinarian's license. You can lodge a complaint against the veterinarian with the appropriate state agency that regulates veterinarians. This is *not* a malpractice lawsuit but rather your challenge that the one who hurt your horse is not competent to practice veterinary medicine.

Advantages:	Easy to do—you may not even need a lawyer. If you succeed, the veterinarian's license to do business could be suspended or revoked (if the veterinarian is found to be seriously incompetent).
Disadvantages:	These proceedings usually do not compensate you, the one bringing the challenge, for your losses.

First, you will need to find the state regulatory board that disciplines veterinarians or has the power to control or suspend their licenses. Your state government can give you this information, or contact your state legislator's office for assistance. Your lawyer might have this information, as well.

Find a basis other than malpractice to sue the veterinarian. Because of the difficulties that come with hiring another veterinarian as an expert witness, you may want to circumvent a malpractice claim completely and instead sue the veterinarian under other non-malpractice legal theories. This can be a risky strategy, and you should discuss it carefully with your lawyer.

Advantages:	Your case is cheaper, and possibly easier, to bring.
Disadvantages:	You may lose your case. In a 1996 case, for example, the Pennsylvania Supreme Court threw out a lawsuit, finding that the case was improperly pursued under other theories when it really should have been brought for veterinary malpractice.

LIABILITY FOR DEFECTIVE PRODUCTS THAT INJURE YOU OR YOUR HORSE

The fly repellant can on the tack store shelf caught your eye with irresistible promises: "Guaranteed Fly Protection for Horses," and "100% Safe—Will Not Harm You or Your Horse." This product, you thought, can't fail. You bought it and tried it immediately.

But fail it did. Just minutes after applying the fly repellant to your horse's glistening coat, you noticed that the flies were gone - but so was your horse's coat. The fly repellant also blistered your hands severely. This terrible ordeal forced you to spend considerable sums of money on veterinary bills and doctor bills, and you lost several days of work. Can someone be liable for what happened?

The answer may be "yes." When people suffer a personal injury or property damage (such as injury to a horse) because of a defective product, they might have a lawsuit for *products liability*. These lawsuits, like the many failed products they involve, can be very complex.

This section covers the many elements of a products liability case, including:

- Your legal rights if a defective product injures you or your horse
- What makes a product "defective" in the eyes of the law
- Who may be liable for a defective product
- The many defenses you can expect from the seller or manufacturer
- What you can do from the moment you suspect that a defective product is to blame for injuries to you or your horse

Legal Rights if a Defective Product Injures You or Your Horse

If a defective product injures you or your horse, someone or some company that makes or sells products might be legally obligated to compensate you for your losses. Your case begins when you claim that a product manufacturer or distributor was *negligent* for placing a defective product on the market, which caused you harm. [See *Equine Law & Horse Sense* for more information on negligence.]

Some states apply a legal theory called "strict products liability," which would require you, the injured person, to prove that a product was dangerously defective and that the defect caused the injury. This section explores the many other types of legal theories that you would raise in a products liability lawsuit.

Manufacturing defects. If the product that injured you was made differently than the others and, as a result, was sold in a dangerous condition, your products liability case might claim that a "manufacturing defect" is to blame. This could occur if, in the previous example, the fly repellant came from a batch that contained the wrong chemicals or wrong mix of chemicals.

Design defects. Products that are inherently dangerous, even when made according to specifications, could have a "design defect." Unlike a manufacturing defect, in which only a small number of a product may be hazardous, all products manufactured with a design defect are equally capable of injuring consumers.

Inadequate product warnings or instructions. Some products liability lawsuits are based on the complete failure to contain warnings, especially warnings that the product could cause adverse reactions or serious harm to people using them.

In other cases, the issue centers on the adequacy of the warning or instruction. Lawsuits have been brought claiming that the product's instructions were inadequate and caused injury. In the example above, there might be liability if the fly repellant's instructions did not clearly state that the product was too caustic to be used directly from the can but must first be diluted with water.

Where required, warnings should be conspicuous and reasonably capable of being noticed by a product's user. However, the law does not require manufacturers to warn of every conceivable problem or risk. Usually there must be proof that the manufacturer knew, or had reason to know, that the product could injure a sizeable number of people. Going back to the example, if you and your horse have unusually sensitive skin, it is possible that the fly repellant manufacturer had no duty to warn you.

Express warranties. Sometimes the product's maker or seller might be liable for an "express warranty" that turns out to be false (or "breached"). An express warranty is a statement of fact or description of the item sold that has formed the basis of the bargain and creates a warranty that the product will conform to the statement. It is often unnecessary to have words "guarantee" and "warrant" to create an express warranty. Therefore, in the example, the words "100% Safe—Will Not Harm You or Your Horse" on the fly repellant can could qualify as an express warranty.

What Qualifies as a Defective Product?

An item might be faulty but, in the eyes of the law, still not qualify as a defective"product" to support a case of products liability. For example, certain services are not considered products in some states. This means you might have legal recourse under other legal theories, such as negligence, against installers or repairmen. Courts in some states have also ruled that horses, as defective as you may believe them to be, do not qualify as "defective products."

Who May Be Liable for Defective Products?

Your products liability lawsuit would target certain businesses or persons as the ones responsible. This means that you would sue the following, only when appropriate:

- Manufacturers of the entire product
- Manufacturers of defective component parts
- Retailers
- Distributors
- Wholesalers

Does this mean you are liable if you sell a used item that is later accused of being defective? If your sale was a chance happening or at your own garage sale, the likely answer is no, if you only sell occasionally. The answer might be different, however, if you are in the business of selling items. You can discuss your own liability with a lawyer knowledgeable of your state's laws.

What Legal Defenses Can Be Raised?

Several defenses may apply, such as:

- The user misused or altered the product beyond the use reasonably anticipated. (Maybe you added another chemical to the fly repellant in an effort to "improve" it, when, in reality, you caused a dangerous chemical reaction.)

- Assumption of risk, comparative negligence, or contributory negligence. [For more information on these defenses and legal theories, see *Equine Law & Horse Sense*.] Keep in mind that the defenses vary with the laws in each state.

Also, it is no longer a defense that only the buyer of the product can sue. Consequently, even if you borrowed a product from a friend, you might be able to sue if it harms you due to a dangerous and defective condition.

Finally, the age-old defense of "caveat emptor" (buyer beware) may have been valid in the 1800s but will likely fail today. With highly sophisticated products on the market, it is virtually impossible for buyers, regardless of how carefully they scrutinize products, to apply the same knowledge of a trained chemist, engineer or scientist.

Can the Product Manufacturer's Written Disclaimer Prevent a Lawsuit?

Not always. A manufacturer's disclaimer is not really a waiver of liability, even though it may look like one.

Sometimes, a seller can legally disclaim or modify certain warranties, and avoid some liabilities associated with their products. The Federal Magnuson-Moss Warranty Act [which is found in title 15 of the United States Code, Sections 2301-2312], addresses how warranties can be disclaimed when they are used in certain consumer products. The law allows a product's limited warranty to apply if it "sets forth in clear and unmistakable language and [is] prominently displayed on the face of the warranty."

Product sellers sometimes use phrases such as "as is" in purchase agreements and sales documents. In some cases, courts have refused to enforce product disclaimers, especially if they have sweeping language designed to eliminate the manufacturer's liability. The manufacturer's reasonable limited warranties, as opposed to a total disclaimer, stand a greater chance of being enforced.

If a Defective Product Harms You, What Can You Do?

Seek medical attention promptly. If you are injured, the most immediate concern will obviously be to attend to your medical needs.

Preserve evidence. If you were the injured fly repellant user in the example, you should store the product in a safe place, without discarding or changing its contents. If you later decide to pursue legal action, the product is prime evidence and will likely receive intense scrutiny from lawyers, experts, and consultants.

Take pictures of the damage. Consider taking photographs or videos of your blistered hand and your horse's burned skin right now, in case you need this evidence later.

Keep product information. Who manufactured the product? Where did you buy it? Is there a serial, model, or identification number? Do you have the instructions that came with the product? Very likely, you will need this information if you elect to pursue legal action.

Possible legal action. If you are considering legal action, consult promptly with a knowledgeable attorney.

183

MIND YOUR MESSAGE—HOW DEFAMATION CAN AFFECT THE HORSE INDUSTRY

John is a successful horse trainer. Maddie, who was new to the horse training business, was struggling to attract clients. One day, desperate to develop business, Maddie made up a nasty rumor that John abused his horses and gave them performance-altering drugs. Maddie knew this was not true. As time went on, the rumor spread. John's customers slowly left his barn, and many of them became Maddie's new customers. Does John have a case against Maddie?

Yes. This section briefly discusses several aspects of the law of defamation. It covers:

- Types of defamation that could apply to you, your horse, or your business
- Who can be sued
- Defenses
- What you can win back from someone who has defamed you or, if you are the one accused of defaming another, what you may have to pay that person

Over the years, a few very serious defamation cases have been fought between people actively involved with horses. Everyone in the horse industry should understand—and avoid—liability for defamation.

What is Defamation?

Defamation occurs when somebody makes a communication (through written words, spoken words, and even e-mails) that is false and tends to lower your reputation in the community or deter others from associating with you. The most common forms of defamation are slander and libel. *Slander* is generally defamation involving spoken words, and *libel* generally involves written words.

A lawsuit for defamation typically involves these elements:

- A false or defamatory statement

- Concerning the "plaintiff" (the one injured by the defamatory communication). For slander or libel, the plaintiff is typically a living person, but this section discusses your rights if your business or even your horse was the target of a false or defamatory statement

- That was actually seen or heard by other people. John has no case if Maddie should call John a crook while nobody else is around, even if Maddie's statement was a lie.

- There was no "privilege" recognized by law to protect you from liability for making the statement. Privileges are discussed below.

- The statement accused of being defamatory has a tendency to harm the plaintiff's reputation, or it did harm the person's reputation

Who Can Be Sued for Defamation?

People who say or publish defamatory statements—and even people connected with these statements—run the risk being sued for defamation, within legally established limits. Those at risk include (but are not limited to) the person who made the statement, others who repeat the statement or circulate the defamatory written material, or the publisher of a magazine or web site that contains defamatory statements about somebody.

Damages

In many cases, the victim of slander or libel does not need to prove that he or she suffered an actual financial loss due to the defamatory statement. In many states, the law will allow these damages to be *presumed* if the complained-of defamatory statement fits within any of these categories:

- The statement attributes the commission of a crime (particularly one involving moral turpitude) to the defamed person

- The statement falsely claims the defamed person had a "loathsome" disease

- The statement accuses the defamed person of highly inappropriate conduct in his or her business or profession

- The statement accuses the defamed person of being "unchaste"

In the example at this section's beginning, because the slander at issue fell into at least one of the above categories, John could bring a case against Maddie without even proving that he suffered a monetary loss, such as a loss of his customers, from Maddie's statements. (Chances are good, though, that he has this proof.) In this setting, many states would allow people like John to recover at least a nominal sum from Maddie, the wrongdoer, as long as he can prove defamation.

What Defenses Are Available?

If you are accused of defaming someone, you have several defenses available to you. Here are some:

Truth. If someone accuses you of making defamatory statements, but your statements were completely true, you have an absolute defense.

Consent. If the person who claims to be defamed actually consented to what you said or wrote, he or she may have no valid claim.

Privilege. A privileged communication is one that is legally justified and is immune to a challenge of defamation, but there are important limits. For example, the law recognizes that statements made in court by lawyers, judges, and witnesses that are reasonably relevant to the legal proceedings are privileged. Sometimes, statements that a person makes, without malice, to appropriate law enforcement agencies can be privileged. If Maddie has a legitimate, good faith basis to believe that John was running afoul of anti-cruelty laws and she notified the police that she personally witnessed him do this, her statements to the police could be privileged. The law regarding privilege can be very complex, and there are exceptions. Your lawyer can discuss it with you.

No malice. Malice can be an important element in defamation cases. Malice, in the setting of a defamation dispute, essentially means that the one making the statement knew it was false when it was made or that he or she had serious doubts about the truth of the statement.

First Amendment. Constitutional rights of free speech will not necessarily protect those who defame others. The law recognizes that limits exist.

The one defamed was a "public figure." If the defamed person legally qualifies as a "public figure" (typically, this classification belongs to a celebrity, high-profile athlete, politician, or another of that stature and prominence), a misstatement that was made honestly and in good faith will typically not support a case. Rather, the public figure must prove that the defaming party acted with "*malice.*"

Opinion. Could Maddie insulate herself from liability for slander by telling others: "John abuses his horses and drugs them illegally, *in my opinion*"? Not always. In some states, statements of opinion, when they include facts that can later be evaluated and proven false (such as Maddie's "facts" that John abuses and drugs horses), could actually support defamation.

Statute of limitations. The statute of limitations for a defamation lawsuit (the time frame in which you can bring suit) can be very short. A lawsuit filed too late, regardless of how meritorious it may seem, risks dismissal for this reason.

Defamation Rights of Your Business, or Even Your Horse

In the typical slander or libel case, the plaintiff (the one who brings the suit) is a living human being who was *personally* defamed. But if your business or even if your *horse* was defamed, you might have other legal rights under theories that look like defamation, but are different. Here are two:

Disparagement. If someone makes false statements that belittle your *business* or something you own (such as your horse), and if those lies were made to keep others from doing business with you, you might have a case against that person for disparagement. A disparagement case is different from a case of slander or libel—you will likely have to prove your actual monetary losses.

Interference with your business contracts or business relationships. If you have business relationships, the law could protect them against unreasonable interference by others. For example, a competitor's business might be answerable to a lawsuit if it deceitfully and wrongfully tried to lure away people who do business with you. The theory is that the wrongdoer intentionally interfered with your business contracts (such as the contracts that John had with his customers) or interfered with your business relationships.

Because states differ on these theories and whether they can be pursued, your lawyer can advise you of your rights and which of them are available to you under your law.

A PICTURE IS WORTH A THOUSAND ... *DOLLARS?* UNDERSTANDING YOUR LEGAL RIGHT OF PUBLICITY

You proudly sit astride your horse, with an ear-to-ear grin, grasping a big blue ribbon. This photograph graces the walls of your home, and it even appeared in a magazine along with a news report of the horse show. One day, however, you noticed that a major equine goods manufacturer is using your picture for its advertisements in magazines—without your permission. Worse yet, the product next to your picture is one that you personally dislike and would never lend your picture to. What are your rights?

Like every person, you have the right to control the commercial use of your identity. This is commonly known as your "right of publicity." This section discusses:

- Your legal rights when others violate your right of publicity for their own business purposes

- Legal defenses available to who are those accused of violating your right of publicity

- How businesses and equine groups can avoid liability pertaining to publicity rights

The Right of Publicity

Someone who uses your name, photograph, or likeness for a business purpose—such as in an advertisement or business promotion—should have your consent. You have the right to deny consent or seek fair compensation in exchange for the use of your name and likeness. Famous athletes, for example, sell their right of publicity to breakfast cereals, phone companies, and numerous other businesses through product endorsements. High profile people in the horse industry, such as John Lyons and George Morris, sell endorsements, too. In the example, if a business uses your likeness to sell its products without your consent, you have a legal basis to claim that your legal rights were violated.

Your right of publicity is well recognized in the law. Certain state and federal laws allow you to sue the wrongdoer and ask for money (the sum of money you seek is called "damages").

State Laws

Many state consumer protection laws (sometimes called deceptive trade practice laws) allow people whose rights were violated to recover their losses. These laws were created to help consumers fight back against "deceptive and unfair trade practices." In the example above, many of these laws would consider the act of using someone's likeness or picture without permission to be an unlawful "deceptive and unfair trade practice."

Deceptive trade practice laws often punish wrongdoers severely. Many of them will require the wrongdoer to pay you back the cost of your legal fees, if you win your case. Some even double or triple the amount of your losses—and make the wrongdoer pay you this much larger amount.

Federal Laws

A federal law called the Lanham Act [United States Code, title 15, Section 1125(a)] also addresses publicity rights. Part of this law states:

> Any person who, in connection with any goods or services ... uses in commerce any word, term, name, symbol, or device, or any combination thereof, or any ... false or misleading description of fact, which ... is likely to cause confusion or to cause mistake, or to deceive as to the affiliation, connection, or association of such person with another person, or as to the origin, sponsorship, or approval of his or her goods, services, or commercial activities by another person ... shall be liable in a civil action by any person who believes that he or she is likely to be damaged by such act.

Like many of the consumer practice laws, the Lanham Act could also force the wrongdoer to pay your legal fees.

What Can the Wrongdoer Do?

If someone has violated your legal rights of publicity, you could demand that the wrongdoer do several things, such as:

Compensate you for the value of your name or likeness. You might be able to seek compensation or royalties that resulted from the wrongdoing.

Stop the advertisements immediately. Chapter Three of this book addressed the law of injunctions as they can apply to horse sales. The fact is, an injunction can also be pursued to stop the wrongdoer from running an advertising or promotional campaign that wrongly uses your photograph or likeness. In the example above, if you disliked the product that had your photograph or likeness next to it, and if you wanted to stop the impression that you approved of the product, your lawyer might want to seek an injunction to quickly stop the ads from running.

These options are not right for all cases, and there are others not mentioned. Your lawyer can discuss your legal options with you.

What Defenses are Available?

In the situation above, here are two of the many defenses that the wrongdoer might assert.

The Infringer Was Exercising its Free Speech Rights. The right of free speech, which is guaranteed by the First Amendment to the U.S. Constitution, is broad but not without limit. Free speech might be a winning defense when, for example, a photographer took your picture and a newspaper printed it along with results from the horse show in which you completed. In this setting, your photograph would arguably be for a *communicative*, newsworthy purpose, and the newspaper would assert that the First Amendment protects it.

The result would be completely different if, as in the example above, the wrongdoer took your photograph and likeness and used it for a *commercial purpose* for its own benefit. If the wrongdoer somehow gained, or sought to gain, a business advantage, then its actions are probably not protected by the First Amendment.

You Consented to the Ads or Gave Up Your Rights. If you agreed to allow a person or business to use your photograph or likeness through a legally valid contract, you would have effectively given up your rights to seek money.

Avoiding Liability

To avoid violating someone's right of publicity, get written permission from the people whose names or pictures you want to use, especially if you plan to use the names or pictures for a *business* or *commercial* purpose. Even if you may have taken the photo—and thus own the copyright—if you use the person's likeness, you are at risk of violating the person's rights.

The best way to get permission is to have the person (or their parents or legal guardians) sign a well-written "publicity waiver." Many equine organizations and show managers do this. Those who sign these documents give the group, or others on its behalf, the right to take your picture and use it to promote its activities or for other purposes.

Conclusion

In conclusion, please keep the following ideas in mind:

1. Not every use of your photograph or likeness, in the eyes of the law, violates your right of publicity. However, where the wrongdoer uses your photograph or likeness for a business purpose, such as in its advertisements or promotions, the chances become greater that your right of publicity has been violated. If you suspect that a violation has taken place, your options are to do nothing (after all, many people *enjoy* the publicity, especially when someone else is paying to publicize you), or contact a lawyer.

2. This section does not address the *value* of a person's right of publicity. Basketball superstar Michael Jordan and figure skating champion Tara Lipinski, for example, sell their endorsements for millions. Obviously, these values reflect, in large part, the unique "celebrity" status and widespread recognition each has achieved. In comparison, the average man and woman in the horse industry cannot expect their publicity rights to be worth a huge amount of money.

3. If you have a winning case, state and federal laws that address violations of publicity rights also allow you to win back your attorney fees, at the wrongdoer's expense.

CHAPTER TEN

EQUINE INSURANCE –
TROUBLE-SAVING
INFORMATION AND TIPS

15 Common Myths
Regarding Equine Insurance

Getting what you pay for—this is everyone's goal, whether it is buying fuel for your vehicles or feed for your horses. Surprisingly, where equine insurance is involved, most people do not understand what they need, what they bought, whether they really have the coverage they think they do, and how to keep their coverage intact.

When it comes to equine-related insurance, myths and misconceptions have plagued the horse industry for years. People fail to read their insurance policies and instead rely on myths, often making costly mistakes. Coverage may be denied because they failed to comply with an important policy condition. Or, in some cases, people learn that the policy they bought offers no coverage for the problem at hand.

Insurance is a very important and expensive purchase. To maximize the value of insurance, I am exposing many of these myths for you. Here are 15 of the most common myths surrounding equine-related insurance.

1. "I No Longer Need Liability Insurance Since My State Has Passed an Equine Activity Liability Law"

Liabilities in the horse industry have changed a great deal over the last decade. As explained in Chapter Seven, as of January 2000, 44 states have passed laws designed to, in some way, limit or control liabilities in horse activities. A list of these states can be found in the Appendix. None of these laws ends liability altogether. As the possibility for liability remains, the need for insurance is strong.

2. "I Need No Insurance Because I Make Everyone Sign a Waiver of Liability"

Having a waiver or release of liability does not eliminate the need for proper insurance. People who sign releases can, and sometimes do, sue. The success or failure of their lawsuits depends on several factors, including whether the applicable state's law enforces releases.

Fortunately, most states do, but it depends on how well the release was drafted and the circumstances under which the release was signed.

Should a lawsuit be brought against you, and if you have no insurance, you are responsible for paying your own legal fees and for paying any settlement or judgment. By comparison, when a lawsuit or claim is covered by insurance, the insurance company will handle the legal defense and, if appropriate, pay, the demand, claim, or judgment up to a specific dollar amount.

3. "My Homeowner's Insurance Policy Covers All Liabilities Arising From My Horse-Related Business Activities"

The standard homeowner's insurance policy is *not* business insurance. Homeowner's policies, by their terms, almost always exclude coverage (and therefore will not protect you) if someone is injured in connection with a "business pursuit." Homeowner's insurance policies likely cover the event when a social visitor, such as a dinner guest, slips and falls near your barn. However, the policy might not protect you if the one who fell was a business customer, such as a boarder.

Numerous activities, such as riding lessons, horse boarding, or horse training, when done in exchange for money or something of value, can qualify as "business pursuits." For these activities, it is important to buy commercial general liability insurance or other insurance that is expressly designed to cover your business activities.

If you are an equine professional, you would be wise to confirm that you are actually insured for your business activities. Read your policy, and talk to your insurance agent.

4. "I Just Bought an Umbrella Policy From My Homeowner's Insurance Agent. Now I am Covered for My Horse-Related Business Activities"

If your existing insurance policy does not cover "business pursuits," your umbrella policy might not cover them, either. Umbrella insurance policies often increase your policy limits on some or all of your existing liability insurance. For example, if your original homeowner's liability insurance policy had limits of $500,000, a $500,000 umbrella policy could bring that total to $1 million. If you believe that your umbrella policy offers coverage for risks beyond your homeowner's insurance, be sure to read the policy carefully or confirm this in writing with your agent or the insurance company.

5. "My Horse Got Sick and Had to Be Put Down. Now I Can Call the Insurance Company That Issued a Mortality Insurance Policy on the Horse"

A common myth is that the mortality insurance company should only be notified *after* your horse's demise. Nothing could be father from the truth. In fact, most mortality insurance policies require "immediate" or "prompt" notice of an insured horse's injury, lameness, or illness. Those who fail to comply with these notice requirements risk losing their mortality insurance coverage.

Because notice requirements can vary from company to company, make sure to read your insurance policy carefully and make reasonable efforts to comply. Keep your insurance company's designated notice number—usually a toll-free (800) number—in a handy place.

6. "When The Time Comes to Notify the Company That Issued My Mortality Insurance Policy, I'll Just Call My Insurance Agent"

Giving notice to the wrong person or entity could be treated the same as giving *no* notice at all. As you check your insurance policy for the name and phone number of the person or company designated to receive notice, you will be surprised to learn that the agent who sold you the insurance is probably not the right one to call when you have a claim. When your horse's condition takes a turn for the worse, make sure that you have quick access to the right telephone number.

7. "I Have Been Sued for Negligently Caring for a Horse that I Board in My Barn, But My Equine Business Liability Insurance Should Cover This"

Not always. Standard equine commercial general liability insurance policies only cover accidents and injuries affecting humans and incidental property damage. If an accident or injury affects only a horse, which is treated as personal property, many of these policies do not cover them.

Commercial general insurance policies would cover a stable in this scenario if the stable bought extra insurance commonly known as "care, custody, and control" insurance (some companies call this insurance "care, custody, *or* control" insurance, or a "bailee's liability policy").

8. "My Equine Business Liability Insurance Covers the Same Thing as Worker's Compensation Insurance"

Not true. Commercial general liability policies almost always exclude injuries to your employees while they are on the job. It takes a policy of worker's compensation insurance to cover these incidents.

9. "My Horse Went Lame After I Bought a Mortality Insurance Policy, But I Can Renew the Policy Next Year Without a Veterinary Examination"

Many insurance companies require an updated veterinary certification as a condition to the annual renewal of a mortality insurance policy. The veterinary certification tells the company that the horse remains in good health.

Other companies may allow automatic policy renewals without the veterinary certification, but this renewal practice is almost always announced in writing. Companies that waive the veterinary certification requirement will still ask you to complete a form attesting to the horse's good condition. If a company's renewal requirements are important to you, evaluate them before buying the insurance.

10. "The Insurance Company Will Pay Me the Full Policy Limits If I Bring a Valid Mortality Insurance Claim After My Horse Dies"

People sometimes misunderstand the amount of the mortality insurance they buy. This misunderstanding arises when they fail to read their policies in order to determine whether they have purchased an "actual cash value" or an "agreed value" policy.

To illustrate the difference between an "actual cash value" and "an agreed value" policy, let's assume that you purchased a mortality insurance policy with a $10,000 face value on the life of a horse. Now, let's follow a claim on that policy. We will assume that you, as the horse's owner, submitted a proper and timely claim, the loss of the horse was covered under the policy's terms, and the insurance company has agreed to pay the claim.

If you purchased an "agreed value" mortality insurance policy, the insurer would pay you the full $ 10,000. "Agreed value" policies provide coverage for a specifically agreed-upon amount.

If you purchased an "actual cash value" or fair market value policy, the insurance company might pay you less than $10,000 if it had reason to believe that the lesser amount reflects the fair market value of your horse around the time of its death.

198

11. "I Can Buy Mortality Insurance in Any Amount, Even if it Exceeds My Horse's Real Value"

Mortality insurance policies are meant to insure the amount your horse would likely command in today's market. To determine the horse's value, the insurance policy application requires truthful disclosure of the amount paid for the horse, the horse's show, race, use or breeding record, health, condition, and other information. The insurance company will rely on this information in determining whether to insure your horse for the amount you request.

12. "My Horse is Sore, But I Can Still Recover 100% of His Value Under a Loss of Use Policy"

Unlikely. Loss of use policies are really not designed to pay 100% of the value of a horse simply because the horse is rendered temporarily disabled.

Unlike mortality insurance, which pays a sum if your horse dies or is stolen, loss of use insurance applies if your horse is alive but suffers from a physical condition that renders it *permanently* unable to perform the specific function for which it was insured (such as showing or racing). Consequently, before they will issue payment under a loss of use policy, insurance companies require proof that the horse is "totally and permanently" unable to fulfill its intended use. Under this standard, a temporary soreness condition will not make your horse a candidate for payment.

Just to confirm that the horse satisfies the "totally and permanently disabled" standard, insurance companies can also require opinions from two veterinarians. Also, if you qualify for payment under a loss of use policy, chances are good that you may be required to surrender your horse—permanently—to the insurance company.

13. "My Major Medical and Surgical Insurance Will Pay All Expenses Involved in Keeping My Horse"

Major medical and surgical insurance is optional extra insurance coverage that many companies offer to those who apply for a mortality insurance policy. Major medical and surgical insurance is designed to pay for surgery and also, up to a certain amount, diagnostic tests, certain non-surgical treatment, and certain other medical care that your horse receives from a licensed veterinarian or veterinary care facility. This type of insurance covers expenses reasonably associated with serious, costly care of a horse, such as colic surgery, but not unrelated costs, such as Coggins tests.

Major medical and surgical insurance policies only pay up to policy limits. Common policy limits for this type of insurance are $5,000 or $7,500. If your out-of-pocket veterinary expenses should exceed your policy's coverage limit, you will be responsible for paying the excess on your own.

14. "The Insurance Policy Our Association Bought to Cover Our Horse Show Insures Us Against Claims That May Be Brought By Spectators and Participants at the Show"

Event liability insurance, which clubs and organizations often buy for events such as shows, races, clinics, or expositions, usually only applies to claims for injury, death, or damage brought by spectators. Unless specifically provided in the policy, this type of insurance may not cover claims brought by event participants, such as competitors in the show.

15. "The Cheaper Insurance is Better"

It always pays to be a smart shopper. While comparing prices on insurance policies, however, keep in mind that the cheaper premium might reflect poorer coverage. Make sure that the policies you are comparing have identical coverage and that the insurance companies are financially sound and reputable.

Conclusion

Your friends or your horse trainer can give useful advice on splint boots, saddle pads, and good horsemanship. Insurance policies, however, are detailed documents, and their provisions can differ from company to company. Stick to the advice of a reputable and knowledgeable insurance agent who understands your needs and knows equine-related insurance very well. Or, seek legal advice.

WHO NEEDS
WORKER'S COMPENSATION INSURANCE?

While driving to the feed store to pick up a load of grain, a barn worker is injured in an automobile accident. Across town, an employee of another stable forgets to keep a safe distance while pasturing a horse and gets kicked in the head. Both have huge medical bills, and it will be months before either can return to work. Who is responsible?

What is Worker's Compensation?

Generally speaking, when employees are injured, ill, or die in the course of their employment, they—or their families or dependents—are usually entitled to collect worker's compensation benefits. The entitlement is virtually automatic, as long as the worker qualifies as an employee and experiences an on-the-job injury.

Worker's compensation laws were enacted to reduce court delays, encourage safety, and give injured employees a reliable source of income and benefits, regardless of who was at fault in causing the injury. The issue of negligence—whether on part of the employer or the worker—plays no part in a worker's compensation matter. This means that the barn worker who was kicked in the head while trying to pasture a horse, even if his own negligence and inattentiveness helped cause the injury, could recover benefits. All 50 states and the federal government now have some type of worker's compensation law in effect.

What Does Worker's Compensation Generally Cover?

If the "employee" suffers an injury, illness, or death on the job, then worker's compensation applies. Benefits, which vary depending on the severity of the injury and whether the injury is permanent, can include reimbursement for medical expenses, doctor bills, hospital stays, and rehabilitation costs. Benefits can also include reimbursement for a certain amount of the worker's lost income. Should a worker die, the laws provide certain benefits to his or her spouse and certain dependents (such as the worker's children).

Other losses, such as "pain and suffering," are generally not recoverable through worker's compensation. However, the injured worker might seek to recover them from others responsible for the injury. (Maybe, for example, a defective machine was at fault and its manufacturer could be sued separately.)

Who Qualifies for Benefits?

Worker's compensation benefits are only available to "employees" (as defined in the applicable law) who suffer illnesses, injuries, or death arising "out of and in the course of employment." In the earlier examples, both the injured driver and stable worker would likely have claims. Those seeking worker's compensation benefits should notify the employer promptly after an injury and, where required, submit a claim form.

Do All Employers Need
Worker's Compensation Insurance?

The laws in your state will tell whether your business needs worker's compensation insurance. Many states require all employers to purchase worker's compensation insurance, unless the employer fits within certain limited exemptions. For example, some exemptions apply to certain farm workers. However, read your laws *very carefully*—stables might not qualify. Other exemptions can include volunteers, family members who help others for free, and those who work for certain non-profit organizations. Very large companies might qualify for the "self-insured" exemption; only the state can decide who qualifies for this and must approve it in advance.

Who Pays for Worker's Compensation Insurance?

Only the employer pays for the worker's compensation insurance, unless it is legally "self-insured" or exempt from the insurance under the law. It is unlawful for any employer to make its workers directly pay for the cost of the worker's compensation insurance coverage.

Which Court Deals With Disputes Involving
Worker's Compensation Insurance?

Disputes often arise involving the amount of worker's compensation benefits, a denial of benefits, or how long the payments will last. If this occurs, these disputes are usually directed not to the local courthouse but rather to a state worker's compensation appeals board (a special body set up by the state). Decisions made by that board can be appealed further, often through the regular court system.

What if a Worker is Injured,
But the Employer is Uninsured?

If your employer fails to purchase worker's compensation insurance and is not legally qualified as "self-insured" or exempt, you the worker might be able to file a lawsuit through the regular court system. In the lawsuit, the employer might be legally responsible for your injuries and losses, but only if the employer was found to be negligent, and the negligence directly caused your injury. State laws might even penalize employers who fail to get proper insurance to cover their injured worker's claims.

Dispelling Common Misconceptions Regarding
Worker's Compensation Insurance

Let's explore some common statements in the horse industry regarding worker's compensation in order to determine which are true and which are not:

- *"My workers are all independent contractors so I don't need to buy worker's compensation insurance."*

True. Independent contractors cannot collect worker's compensation insurance from those who hire them.

However, many equine businesses wrongly assume that their workers are "independent contractors" when, in the eyes of the law, they are not. As explained in *Equine Law & Horse Sense*, if you cannot tell whether the worker is an employee or an independent contractor, the Internal Revenue Service has issued regulations that can help.

- *"While working for someone else one day, I cut my finger a little, but now I can make a worker's compensation claim and collect money for my 'pain and suffering.'"*

False as to the "pain and suffering." Worker's compensation laws are generally *not* designed to pay injured workers a special sum of money to compensate them for their "pain and suffering" associated with their work-related injuries.

- *"I do not need to buy worker's compensation insurance because all of my barn workers know very well the risks that come with working around horses; they have assumed the risk by agreeing to work for me."*

False. An assumed risk does not excuse employers from a duty to secure worker's compensation insurance. With worker's compensation, the negligence of the employer, or even the negligence of the employee, becomes irrelevant. Even if the worker shares some of the blame for negligently failing to look out for his or her safety, such as the earlier example of the stable worker pasturing the horse, the worker may still be legally entitled to collect worker's compensation benefits.

- *"My stable's general business liability insurance will cover claims that any of my workers may bring against me if they are hurt on the job."*

Not necessarily. In fact, most stables' commercial general liability insurance policies, by their terms, *exclude* (and will not protect stables from) claims brought by employees who are hurt on the job. Those insurance policies almost always expect the business to buy worker's compensation insurance. Consequently, unless your stable liability insurance policy expressly covers you for claims from injured workers, you will need to buy extra insurance for worker's compensation. Discuss this with your insurance agent.

MAXIMUM PROTECTION WITH
UMBRELLA INSURANCE

*A casual trail ride turns tragic. Your neighbor, who in-
sisted that she was a highly experienced rider and could handle
Charger, your temperamental horse, turned out to have almost no riding experience. By the time you discovered the truth,
it was too late. While riding at an uncontrolled gallop your
neighbor fell off. She spent several months in the hospital and
can no longer walk. This, combined with head injuries she
sustained in the fall, guarantees that your neighbor will probably
need round-the-clock care for the rest of her life. She sued you,
and she won. A jury issued a $1.5 million verdict against you.
You were not insured for that amount, and now her lawyers
have threatened to take away your home, possessions, and a
huge percentage of your paychecks for many years to come.
Could you have prevented this?*

Can you afford to pay a $1.5 million verdict? Most of us with horses
do not have that kind of money in the bank. But we *do* have the ability
to buy liability insurance. If you are willing to buy a liability insurance policy that will protect you from horse-related lawsuits and
judgments of up to $1 million (sometimes even more than that), insurance
companies will sell it to you. If you want to double that protection,
so that you are protected for up to $2 million, or more, many insur-
ance companies will sell you extra insurance called *umbrella liability
insurance* coverage.

Umbrella insurance is not for everyone. Few people with horses
have it, and judgments or lawsuit settlements of $2 million dollars
or more are rare, but the risk is always there. The extra protection
could save your home, farm, and everything you own if someone has
a legitimate claim against you for a serious personal injury. Because
of this, it helps to know about this insurance and, if you are interested, discuss it with your agent. This section explores umbrella liability
insurance coverage. You will learn:

- What this insurance is and what it does
- What it can cost

- What to consider as you decide whether this insurance is right for you
- Problems to avoid if you buy umbrella insurance

What is Umbrella Insurance?

If you already have liability insurance, you can also buy extra coverage called umbrella insurance; the two work together. That is, your existing liability insurance coverage (sometimes called "primary coverage") remains in place and protects you if someone claims to be injured as a result of your negligence or legal liability. Your umbrella liability insurance coverage only becomes involved when a claim brought against you exceeds the limits of the primary coverage.

Why do companies call the extra coverage "umbrella insurance"? The term "umbrella" refers to the fact that this kind of coverage is a separate policy on top of any other primary insurance coverage you may have.

Here is how the two insurance policies work together. For example, let's say that you purchased a liability insurance policy with $500,000 policy limits, and the policy protects you from injuries someone may sustain as a result of your horse or horse activities. Generally speaking, you are now protected from claims covered by that policy up to $500,000. Let's say that you bought a $1 million umbrella policy on top of that. Assuming that the umbrella policy covers you for the same horse-related accidents or injuries, you now have a total of $1.5 million in insurance coverage.

Is Umbrella Coverage Expensive?

Surprisingly, umbrella insurance policies are *not* expensive. $1 million of umbrella coverage might cost as little as $140 to $250 a year. The cost will vary depending on where you live, and many other factors. The low price reflects the fact that you will probably not need the insurance.

How to Evaluate the Need for Umbrella Coverage

Should you buy umbrella insurance? The decision is yours. As you decide, consider some of the risks that make umbrella insurance coverage worth your serious thought:

The risk of seriously hurting or killing someone in a car accident. The vast majority of umbrella insurance claims come from automobile accidents. This makes umbrella coverage more desirable to those who spend a great deal of time driving on the road.

The risk that someone could blame a severe and disabling injury on you. If someone claims to have suffered a severe and disabling injury because of something you did or failed to do, this claim will test the limits of any ordinary policy of insurance. One example is a "closed head injury," (which usually means a severe and disabling injury to the brain). In some situations, people who experience severe closed head injuries cannot think or walk normally; some remain in comas for years or for the rest of their lives. Consequently, people with closed head injuries run huge medical bills that might even meet or exceed $1 million dollars in the first year alone. This risk—no matter how small it is—gives equine professionals, or others who want to protect themselves from a lawsuit, an incentive to consider umbrella coverage.

The risk that someone might threaten to take away your hard earned money and assets. Wealthy people have every reason to protect their hard-earned personal assets. They know they can pay a $1.5 million judgment but would rather have their insurance company do this for them, at its expense, so that their money and belongings stay where they are. Umbrella insurance offers this peace of mind.

Problems to Avoid When Buying Umbrella Coverage

Make sure that your umbrella insurance policy protects you for the same horse-related risks that your "primary" insurance policy covers. Possibly, a basic umbrella liability insurance policy might not cover the same risks covered by your primary policy. That is, if you purchased a personal horse owner's liability insurance policy (sometimes called a "private horse owner's liability insurance policy") with the aim of protecting you if your horse hurts someone, make sure that your umbrella policy cover these risks too. Your agent can discuss this with you.

Make sure to keep proper coverage in the "primary policy." Certain umbrella insurance policies *require* that you maintain a minimum level of primary insurance at all times, or else you could lose your umbrella coverage. Discuss this with your insurance agent; these requirements often affect your automobile liability coverage.

CHAPTER ELEVEN

ASSOCIATION AND ORGANIZATION LEGAL ISSUES

PROTECTING THE VOLUNTEER WORK FORCE
FROM LIABILITY

Volunteers are the life blood of the horse industry. They make things work. They help run horse shows, handicapped riding programs, associations, 4-H groups, scouting groups, pony clubs, humane societies, and more. Their assistance helps groups perform worthwhile activities smoothly and within budget.

But often, clubs suffer for the lack of volunteers. When asked, members say they worry about getting sued if someone is hurt. The Gallup organization, in a study of volunteerism, noted that one of seven non-profit agencies eliminated one or more programs chiefly in response to a perceived threat of exposure to lawsuits.

In recent years, in an apparent attempt to control liability, the federal government and about half the states have passed laws designed to protect in some way volunteers and/or organizations. In this section, we will explore the laws that are bringing back volunteers by reducing their risk of liability.

State and Federal Laws
That Protect Volunteers From Liability

Federal Law. In 1997, the Federal Volunteer Protection Act took effect. You can find the law in the United States Code, title 42, beginning at Section 14501. First and foremost, this law protects volunteers who assist non-profit groups or certain charitable entities. These people stand to be immune from liability if, during their volunteer tasks, they hurt someone in a negligent way. [The term "negligence" is explained in *Equine Law & Horse Sense*].

You qualify as a "volunteer" under the Volunteer Protection Act if you donate your time to a qualified group that can be either:

- A non-profit organization established under Section 501(c)(3) of the Internal Revenue Code for tax-exempt status (which is discussed later in this chapter); or

- A group that may not have this formal status but is not-for-profit and organizes and conducts itself for charitable, civic, educational, religious, welfare, or other qualified purposes.

As you can see, the federal law was designed to encourage people to volunteer for groups of all sizes—ranging from the United Way to possibly even the neighborhood Saddle and Sirloin Club.

If your group fits within the proper category, the next question is whether you (the worker) are a "volunteer." You can serve the group as an officer, director, trustee, or direct service volunteer. The law considers you a volunteer if you are not paid or given anything worth over $500 for your service; if the group reimburses your expenses, you may still qualify.

The federal law protects volunteers who:

- Act within the scope of their duties when someone got hurt
- Are licensed or otherwise authorized to perform the volunteer activities
- Do not engage in willful or criminal misconduct, gross negligence, or reckless misconduct
- Are not operating a motor vehicle or other vehicle for which the state laws specifically require the volunteer to have an operator's license or have some sort of insurance in effect.

As an example, let's take the ribbon and trophy bearer at the local 4-H horse show. She might benefit from this law if she accidentally dropped a first-place trophy on a competitor's head and caused an injury. The law might not protect her, however, if she forcefully threw the trophy at the winner; the injured person might claim that her rage amounted to "willful misconduct" or some other type of wrongdoing that cannot immunize the volunteer.

The Volunteer Protection Act has some exceptions, which allow liability if the volunteer commits violent crimes, acts of terrorism, hate crimes, sex offenses, violations of civil rights laws, or certain other inappropriate acts that volunteers may commit while under the influence of alcohol or drugs. The law also prevents injured people from collecting punitive damages against a volunteer, unless the volunteer acted willfully, criminally, or in conscious indifference to the rights of the injured person.

State Laws. In an effort to encourage volunteerism, many states have enacted volunteer immunity statutes. All the laws differ in their coverage and scope. Some of the laws narrowly protect volunteer officers and directors who assist non-profit corporations. Other laws are much broader to protect any person who merely performs volunteer services for a group. Make sure to read your state's law very carefully.

It is possible that your state law might offer you less protection from liability than the Federal Volunteer Protection Act. However, the federal law was designed to preempt (take priority over) inconsistent state laws, except when those state laws offer immunities to volunteers that are even broader than the federal law. There are other limits, which you can discuss with your lawyer.

Defenses Available to Groups When Sued

Just because a volunteer may enjoy protection does not mean that the group will be lawsuit-free. Groups face the prospect of liability and should take precautions to plan ahead. When a group faces a lawsuit because a volunteer has hurt someone, here are some of the defenses available to the group:

The group had no control over the volunteer. In some states, if the group had no control over the volunteer worker and what the worker does, then it is possible that the group should not be found legally responsible for the worker's negligent acts. "Control" is, in some cases, determined by how often the volunteer donates his time to the group, and how extensively the group directed the volunteer to do the work.

The volunteer was not doing volunteer work when someone else got hurt. If the volunteer was not acting "within the scope of employment" or was simply not doing volunteer duties when someone else got hurt, then it follows that the organization should not face the consequences of the volunteer's negligence. In the earlier example of the ribbon and trophy bearer, some states might spare the club from liability on the basis that she was not acting "within the scope of his employment" when she hit the winner with the trophy.

The culprit was not a volunteer. The group should not be responsible for the actions of persons who do not even qualify as volunteers.

Suggestions to Help Groups Avoid Liability

If you have volunteers in your work force, here are a few ideas to avoid liability:

Get, and read, a copy of the Federal Volunteer Protection Act and your state law (if one exists). Also, find out if your state has enacted a volunteer immunity law and how it applies to your group's operations.

Consider giving basic training to your volunteers. For many groups, the issue of training volunteer workers seems like a double-edged sword. That is, some groups avoid training their volunteers for fear that the training efforts, in themselves, would reflect a degree of control over workers and potentially increase the group's exposure to liability if a trained worker does improper acts. Depending on the group's activities, however, the group may still be obligated to give some training to its volunteer workers, *especially* if the volunteer activities carry some degree of risk.

Some groups "accredit" or certify their volunteer workers, after these workers pass a special program of instruction. Giving out this accreditation is the group's way of assuring that the volunteer had sufficient training on how to work safely and capably.

Consider, with legal counsel, delegating volunteer training to a specially-created "sub-agency." In an effort to limit their liability for the negligent acts of volunteers, some organizations establish their own "sub-agencies" that do not answer to the organization's main branch but supervise volunteer activities directly. This keeps the main branch away from these tasks. A structure like this can be very complex; the sub-agency should be a legitimate, independent entity and not a sham calculated only to avoid liability—the latter could be rejected by a court and the main branch could face the very liabilities it tried to avoid. Groups considering this structure should consult with their attorneys.

Assign duties with care. Assign volunteers to duties within their capabilities. Consider, for example, the volunteer's age, common sense, strength, and the degree of supervision that he or she will need while doing volunteer work.

Insure yourself. In all situations, organizations should consider buying appropriate insurance to cover volunteer activities. Read on in this section about several types of insurance coverages available to groups.

Dispelling The Myths
Regarding Non-profit Corporations

Non-profit corporations are often misunderstood. These entities are regulated heavily by tax laws, state corporation laws, postal regulations, and by certain immunity laws. This section briefly examines:

- What is a non-profit corporation?
- How non-profit corporate entities differ from for-profit entities
- Myths surrounding non-profit entities, and the facts

What Is a Non-Profit Corporation?

A non-profit corporation is a corporate entity established under federal regulations. The United States Code, title 26, Section 501, states that certain non-profit organizations, if they qualify, are exempt from paying federal income taxes.

Common Features Shared By Non-Profit and For-Profit Corporations

For-profit corporations, such as General Motors, and non-profit corporations, such as the North American Riding for the Handicapped Association, share some common characteristics. For example:

- Shareholders, officers, directors, and members of these entities are protected from any personal liability for any debts or obligations that the entity may incur in its business operations.
- Both entities can earn a profit from their corporate activities. Many non-profit corporations earn very substantial profits.
- In both entities, the membership (or, with a corporation, shareholders) usually elect the board of directors.

How Non-Profit Corporations Differ From For-Profit Corporations

For-profit and non-profit corporations differ in many respects. Here are some factors that make them different:

215

Investors own for-profit corporations and are entitled to a share of the corporations' profits; contributors/investors in non-profit entities are not entitled to a share of the corporation's profits. For-profit corporations issue shares of stock to those who have become eligible by investing money, valuable goods, property, or past services to the entity. These stock shares hold value, especially if the shares can be re-sold or if the corporation pays dividends (payments that represent a share of the corporation's profits) to shareholders. By comparison, non-profit corporations generally cannot issue stock to shareholders. This means that the non-profit corporation does not distribute income to its officers, directors and members.

Non-profit entities may be eligible for federal tax benefits. Many non-profit associations are exempt from paying federal income taxes. To receive federal tax-exempt status under the Internal Revenue Code, Section 501(c)(3), non-profit corporations must limit their purposes to religious, charitable, scientific, testing for public safety, literary, educational, fostering national or amateur sports competition, or preventing cruelty to children or animals. Your lawyer and accountant can discuss this with you.

Postage benefits for certain non-profit mailings. Non-profit entities might qualify for reduced postage rates.

Tax benefits for those who donate to non-profits. In many cases, those who donate money or things (such as used cars) to qualified non-profit entities can deduct the donation from their federal income taxes.

Non-Profit Corporation Myths

Myth 1: Non-profit entities cannot be sued
Fact: They can be sued

The rule of "charitable immunity" began well over 150 years ago under British law, when charitable corporations could not be sued by people who claimed to be injured from the entity's activities. But that was years ago. In recent years, the charitable immunity theory has become largely obsolete. Most states have, in fact, rejected it. Consequently, non-profit entities can be, and sometimes are, sued.

Myth 2: Non-profit entities need no insurance
Fact: They may need several insurance coverages

Because non-profit entities face the risk of being sued, they can protect themselves with different types of insurance. The need for any coverage depends on the group's activities, its state laws, and other factors. Here are some coverages available:

- *Director's and Officer' Liability (often called "D & O" Insurance).* This coverage generally protects directors and officers from a claim or suit relating to the entity's management. For example, the coverage would likely apply if the board of directors, in good faith, decided to fire an employee but later got sued.

- *General Liability.* This insurance will protect against claims or suits that arise out of the entity's business activities. While these policies typically protect the entity only, you can ask your insurance agent to extend coverage to protect the volunteers, as well.

- *Worker's Compensation.* The previous chapter discussed this coverage. Your insurance agent or lawyer can explain whether your state law requires this coverage for your entity.

- *Commercial Automobile Insurance.* If, for example, a non-profit equine rescue group owned its own truck, auto-related coverage would be important. Also, because different volunteer workers will likely drive the truck, the group can require volunteers to have their own separate coverage and to show proof that they are qualified, licensed drivers.

- *Medical Coverage.* Groups can buy medical coverage to protect their volunteers, if they are hurt while helping out.

- *Event Insurance.* General Liability insurance might exclude coverage for a group's events, especially if they involve horses or animals. Check your policy and secure extra coverage when needed. As discussed in this book, be aware that some event policies might not protect against a claim or suit brought by an injured participant.

Myth 3: **Membership on a non-profit board of directors requires little time**

Fact: **Because of the many tasks required, the time commitment can be huge**

Directors of non-profit entities have major responsibilities, which usually translate into plenty of work and long hours. Directors' tasks can include:

- Attending director meetings as often as possible and voting on the non-profit entity's business matters

- Reading and approving minutes and other documents that are presented at board meetings

- Establishing and approving the entity's budget and financial documents, such as banking and accounting records

• Hiring staff, legal counsel, and accountants, when needed

These are only a few of the volunteer directors' many tasks. Board membership usually involves working on several committees and organizing or assisting projects.

Myth 4: **Liability insurance, in particular, is unnecessary now that laws commonly exist that protect non-profit organizations and their officers and directors from liability**

Fact: **These laws do not eliminate the need for insurance**

Many state and federal laws do exist that create immunities from liability for volunteer officers and directors of non-profit organizations. These laws, much like equine activity liability laws, are not "zero liability laws." Many immunize the group from liability unless its volunteers commit intentional wrongdoing, serious misconduct (called "wanton and willful misconduct"), or gross negligence. The mere threat of these types of lawsuits, regardless of whether the suits are well-founded, is reason enough to keep appropriate insurance in place.

Myth 5: **Non-profit entities can enjoy the reduced-cost non-profit postage rate regardless of what they include in their mailings**

Fact: **Reduced-cost mailing privileges can be lost, depending on what the mailings include**

Non-profit entities are eligible for reduced cost mailing privileges. However, United States Postal Service regulations indicate that non-profit entities can lose these privileges if the mailings include advertising for:

• Insurance

• Travel arrangements

• Financial instruments, such as credit cards

Discuss these regulations with your lawyer. For more information, contact the United States Postal Service for its booklet, publication 417, called *Non-Profit Standard Mail Eligibility: Nonprofit and Other Qualified Organizations.*

Myth 6: **Non-profit entities can "lobby" or actively influence state, federal or local legislators**

Fact: **Yes, but within legal limits**

Federal regulations in the Internal Revenue Code indicate that a non-profit corporation organized under Section 501(c)(3) of that

Code could lose its tax-exempt status if a "substantial part" of its activities are directed to actively influencing legislation (a practice generally known as "lobbying"). Under the tax laws, "lobbying" is an attempt to influence legislation by propaganda or otherwise. Examples include: communicating with a legislator who is involved in forming legislation, or participating in a political campaign. Also, a non-profit organization's communications to its members regarding pending legislation could be considered lobbying.

Some non-profit organizations that do a sizeable amount of lobbying protect their non-profit status by removing themselves entirely from lobbying and establishing separate entities—often called Political Action Committees—for the lobbying and political efforts. Discuss this with your lawyer.

Myth 7:   **Non-profit corporations cannot make a profit**

Fact: **These entities often earn huge profits, but cannot share them with their officers, directors, and members**

As explained earlier, non-profit corporations can raise tremendous amounts of money, and many do. However, non-profit corporations cannot distribute their income or profits to their officers, directors, and members.

CHAPTER TWELVE

GLOSSARY OF LEGAL TERMS

GLOSSARY OF LEGAL TERMS

Action A legal dispute handled through the court system. Related terms: case or lawsuit.

Affidavit A written statement of a witness in a legal proceeding that is made or signed under an oath.

Agent One who carries on certain lawful activity on behalf of another (the principal), subject to the principal's direction. Opposite term: principal.

Agister's Lien A security interest in another person's horse to secure the payment of a debt that arises from the care and keeping of the horse. Related term: Stablemen's lien.

Appeal A request that a higher court review a decision issued by a lower level court to find errors or irregularities.

Arbitration A process by which a legal dispute is resolved out of court with a neutral person or panel of persons hearing both sides of a case, examining certain evidence, and then rendering a decision that may or may not be binding.

Attractive Nuisance A dangerous condition on or of someone's land that, by its features, has the ability to attract young children onto the property.

Bailment A legal relationship that exists when, for example, a horse owner (the "bailor") leaves a horse with the boarding stable ("bailee") for care and keeping. In this setting the stable must give the horse reasonable care.

Bar A lawyer organization.

Bond A guarantee that someone will fully perform an obligation to another, as evidenced in a payment of money (sometimes kept with a court or somewhere else). If the performance does not follow, then the non-performing person's money is released.

Breach (of Duty or of Contract) A departure, without legal justification, from conduct that is expected based on a legal standard or from an obligation that was created by a contract.

Case Law The law established by decisions of courts, as opposed to statutes or other sources.

Caveat Emptor A phrase meaning "let the buyer beware," which represents a rule of law in the 1800s that people buy at their own risk.

Claim A legal demand or assertion. When a person asserts through a legal proceeding that another owes him money or has some other legal obligation, that person has brought a claim.

Class Action Lawsuit brought by one or more individuals on behalf of a larger group of people who are in the same legal situation.

Code A law established by a legislative body such as a state house of representatives or senate. Related term: statute.

Complaint The plaintiff's first filing that begins a lawsuit. The Complaint sets forth the plaintiff's claims against the defendant. Related term: petition.

Consideration Something of value that is given in exchange for the other party's promise to fulfill a promise.

Contract A legally-enforceable promise between two or more parties who have exchanged consideration.

Counsel Lawyers in a case; legal advice.

Counter-claim A claim brought against a plaintiff by a defendant in a lawsuit. In the counterclaim, the defendant sues the plaintiff. Related terms: crossclaim; third-party claim.

Crossclaim A claim made by a defendant in a case against another defendant. Related terms: counterclaim; third-party claim.

Damages When a person believes he or she has suffered some sort of loss due to the wrongful actions of another, the monetary compensation allowed by law is known as damages.

Decree Judicial command. Related term: mandate.

Default Failing to carry out a legal obligation, such as show up in court or pay back a loan on time.

Defendant   The party against whom a lawsuit is filed. In a criminal case, the defendant is the one accused of committing a crime. Opposite term: plaintiff.

Deposition   Out of court testimony taken under oath of a party or witness in a lawsuit, with a court reporter or stenographer simultaneously recording a transcript of the testimony.

Discovery   The exchange of information in a lawsuit between the parties.

Disparagement   A claim similar to defamation that may arise if someone makes false statements involving a business or something else.

Express Warranty   An assertion of fact or promise relating to the quality or condition of the item sold that becomes the basis of the bargain.

Federal Case   A case filed in a Federal Court, which, by law, must involve either: (1) a legal dispute between residents of two or more different states and the amount of $75,000 or more in controversy; or (2) an alleged violation of a U.S. Constitutional right (such as a First Amendment freedom of speech) or a federal statute (such as the Americans With Disabilities Act, etc.).

Finding   A conclusion reached by a judge or a jury.

Fraud   The deceptive words or conduct of a person, upon which another person has relied to his or her detriment, which is designed to deprive the other person of money or something of value.

Garnishment   Proceedings through which a creditor who has a judgment against a defendant can seize certain of the defendant's wages or property in order to pay the debt created by the judgment.

General Partnership   A form of business partnership between two or more people, who agree to share in the profits or losses of the business.

Hearing   A legal or governmental proceeding where issues are heard and testimony is sometimes taken.

Hearsay   Second-hand evidence in which a witness has repeated statements made by others.

Holding   A judge's legal conclusion.

Indemni-fication	An arrangement in which someone agrees to compensate another for an anticipated loss or liability. Some indemnification agreements provide that Person A agrees to pay the legal fees or expenses of Person B in the event that a lawsuit is ever brought against Person B due to the wrongful acts of Person A.
Injunction	A court order that either requires a party to undertake a specified act or prohibits a party from carrying out an act.
Installment Payments	Payments spread out over time.
Issue	A point of dispute between two parties in a legal matter.
Joint Venture	A type of partnership that is created for a limited or specific purpose.
Jurisdiction	A court's power to hear and decide a legal dispute.
Lawsuit	A legal action brought by a plaintiff against a defendant in a court of law.
Lessee	One who has received the property of another for a certain period of time. Opposite term: lessor.
Lessor	One who leases out property to another for a certain period of time. Opposite term: lessee.
Liable	Having legal responsibility.
Libel	A written publication such as a book, sign, photograph, or other type of writing that injures a person's character or reputation. Related term: slander.
Limited Partnership	A form of partnership with general partners and limited partners.
Litigant	An individual or business entity involved in a legal dispute. Related terms: plaintiff, defendant, or party.
Litigation	A lawsuit, or the process of handling a lawsuit.
Mandate	Judicial command. Related term: decree.
Mediation	A process in which two disputing parties agree to allow a neutral person or panel of persons to evaluate the dispute and to persuade the parties to settle their differences.
Minor	Someone under the legal age in which the law deems them competent to make certain decisions or sign legal documents. Most states have established that minors are under the age of 18.

Motion	Request that the judge take a certain action.
Municipality	A local government entity such as a city, village, or township.
Negligence	An allegation that another person fell below an established standard designed to protect another from an unreasonable risk of harm. The doing of some act which a person of ordinary prudence would not have done under similar circumstances.
Notary Public	A public officer capable of administering oaths and performing other official acts. In many states, a Notary Public must observe witnesses or parties sign official or important documents.
Nuisance	The use of property or a condition of land that substantially interferes with the use and enjoyment of another's property.
Nuisance Lawsuit	A lawsuit brought by one or more nearby landowners seeking to end or abate the nuisance in some way. The words "nuisance lawsuit" have also been applied over the years to describe any type of lawsuit that is brought without justification and serves as an annoyance or nuisance to the one against whom the suit is brought.
Opinion	A decision issued by a court.
Ordinance	A law passed by a municipal entity, which typically involves zoning and land use, building, and matters of public safety.
Party or Parties	The individuals or business entities involved in a legal dispute. Related terms: plaintiff, defendant, or litigant.
Petition	The plaintiff's first filing that begins a lawsuit. Related term: Complaint.
Piercing the Corporate Veil	A legal theory that would hold the shareholders of a corporation personally liable for certain of the corporation's activities or obligations.
Plaintiff	One who brings a lawsuit against another.
Precedent	Previous legal decisions that guide subsequent cases.

Presumption A rule of law allowing the court to derive inferences from evidence of a certain type until the truth of an inference has been disproved. For example, many courts will presume that a properly-addressed letter placed in a mail receptacle will arrive at its destination within a certain period of time; the recipient must prove otherwise.

Principal Where an agency relationship is involved, a principal is one who has permitted or directed another person (known as the "agent") to act for his benefit and under his supervision and control. Opposite term: agent.

Private Nuisance A lawsuit alleging nuisance liability brought by a nearby landowner. Related term: public nuisance.

Preliminary injunction A type of injunction a court has the power to issue.

Principal A person for whom an agent acts. Related term: agent.

Promissory Note A written document in which a borrower acknowledges a debt and promises payment to the lender under certain terms.

Pro se Representing yourself in a lawsuit. Related terms: *In pro per*.

Proximate Cause The legally sufficient connection between a person's negligence and another person's injury.

Public Nuisance A lawsuit alleging nuisance liability brought by a group of nearby landowners. Related term: private nuisance.

Puffery General statements of sales talk or boasting.

Quorum The number of people who must be present before an action can be taken.

Registered Agent The person whom a corporation selects to receive correspondence and lawsuit papers on its behalf.

Release of Liability A document in which a person of legal age agrees to give up a right or claim against another. Related term: waiver.

Repossess Taking back something of value because the other party has failed to fulfill obligations.

Rescission A legal remedy in which a court cancels a contract as if it were never made.

Ruling A judge's decision.

Security Interest	An interest in property or something that a borrower might give to a lender so that the buyer can obtain that property with payments over time.
Settlement	An agreement by which the parties dispose of a lawsuit or a dispute.
Slander	Spoken words that injure a person's character or reputation. Related term: libel.
Small Claims Court	A court which provides an expeditious and informal way of resolving minor claims. The parties usually represent themselves, but most states allow lawyers to be present.
Specific Performance	A legal action that asks the court to order someone to take a specific action.
Stablemen's Lien	See agister's lien.
Standard of Care	The degree of care that a person should take to protect another's person or property, which can be set by law, typically as reasonable care, or by contract.
Statute	A law established by a legislative body such as congress or a state house or senate body. Related term: code.
Statute of Limitations	The time period allowed by law for a party to bring certain types of claims in a court of law or legal proceeding against a defendant. After this time period has passed, no lawsuit can be filed.
Summons	A formal, written notice advising a defendant that he or she has been sued and/or must appear in court or respond to the lawsuit within a stated time period.
Supreme Court	In most states, this is the highest court to which an appeal can be taken. This is the highest court in the federal government.
Temporary Restraining Order	A type of injunction designed to keep things as they are for a short period of time.
Third-party Claim	A claim made by a defendant in a case against a person or entity who was not originally named as a party in the lawsuit; the defendant commences a third-party claim when he or she brings claims against that party and brings that party into the lawsuit. Related terms: counter-claim; crossclaim.

Tort   A wrong that was committed upon the person or property of another, for which the law recognizes a right to bring suit. A tort is not a violation of a contract.

Trespasser One who enters the property of another without permission or legal justification.

Use Tax   A tax that can be imposed, for example, when someone buys personal property (such as a saddle) out-of-state but later brings it into the taxing state to be stored, used, or consumed.

Usury   Charging an unlawfully high interest rate.

Venue   The county or location in which a court with jurisdiction can hear and decide a legal dispute.

Verdict   The jury's decision.

Waiver   The relinquishment of a right or claim against another. Many states allow a party to waive the right to sue for certain acts or ordinary negligence of another. The waiver can be done in writing or by a course of conduct. Related terms: release of liability.

Warranty   A statement that is made in writing or verbally upon which another relies that forms the basis of a sale; usually, the statement is that the product or thing being sold has certain qualities, such as: "The horse does not crib" or "The horse has never taken a lame step in his life." Related terms: express warranty.

Witness   One who gives testimony under oath about something he or she knew, saw, or heard that is relevant to a lawsuit.

Zoning   Regulations issued by municipal entities such as cities, villages, or townships that indicate how real property can be used in different areas and for different purposes.

EQUINE ACTIVITY LIABILITY LAWS WITH SIGN POSTING AND CONTRACT LANGUAGE REQUIREMENTS (AS OF JANUARY 2000)

APPENDIX
EQUINE ACTIVITY LIABILITY LAWS
(As of January 2000)

State	Citation	Sign Posting Requirement	May Affect Contract &Release Language
Alabama	Code of AL 1975 §6-5-337	X	X
Arizona	AZ Rev. Stat. §12-553		X
Arkansas	AR Code Ch. 120, §16-120-201, *et seq.*	X	
Colorado	CO Rev. Stats. §13-21-119	X	X
Connecticut	CT Gen. Stat. Anno. § 52-557 p		
Delaware	1995 DE Code Title 10, Ch. 81, §8140	X	X
Florida	1993 FL Laws Ch. 93-169, §773.01, *et seq.*	X	X
Georgia	Code of GA Anno. §62-2701	X	X
Hawaii	1994 HI A.L.S. 249		
Idaho	ID Code 1990 Ch. 18, §6-1801, *et seq.*		
Illinois	745 ILC.S.A. § 47/1	X	X
Indiana	IN Stat. Anno. § 34-31-5-1, *et seq.*	X	X
Iowa	IA Code Anno. § 673.1, *et seq.*	X	X
Kansas	1994 KS A.L.S. 290	X	X
Kentucky	KY Rev. Stat. § 247.401, *et seq.*	X	X
Louisiana	LA Rev. Stat. § 9:2795.1	X	X
Maine	ME Stat. Title 7 §4101, *et seq.*	X	X
Massachusetts	MA Gen. Laws 128 §2D	X	X
Michigan	MI C.L. §691.1661, *et seq.*	X	X
Missouri	MO R.S. §537.325	X	X
Minnesota	MN Ch. 623, Art. 3§2	X	

State	Citation	Sign Posting Require- ment	May Affect Contract &Release Language
Mississippi	MS Code Anno. § 95-11-1, *et seq.*	X	X
Montana	MT Code Anno. §27-1-725		
Nebraska	Rev. Stat. of NE § 25-21,249, *et seq.*	X	X
New Hampshire	NH Rev. Stat. Anno. § 508:19		
New Jersey	NJ Stat. 5:15-1, *et seq.*	X	
New Mexico	NM Stat. Anno. Art. 13, §42-13-1, *et seq.*	X	
North Carolina	Gen. Stats. Of NC, ch. 99E, art. 1	X	X
North Dakota	ND Code §53-10-1		
Ohio	OH Rev. Code § 2305.32.1		X
Oklahoma	OK Stat. Title 76 § 50.1, *et seq.*		X
Oregon	OR Rev. Stat. §30.687, *et seq.*		X
Rhode Island	RI Laws Ch. 21, §4-21-1	X	X
South Carolina	SC Laws §47-9-710	X	X
South Dakota	SD Laws Anno. §42-11-1	X	X
Tennessee	TN Code Anno. §44-20-101	X	X
Texas	TX Code Anno. § 87.001, *et seq.*	X	X
Utah	UT Code Anno. §78-27b-101		
Virginia	VA Code Ch. 27.5, §3.1-796.130		X
Vermont	12 VT Stat. Anno. § 1039	X	X
Washington	WA R.C.W 4.24.530		
West Virginia	WV Code Art. 4 § 20-4-1		X
Wisconsin	WI S.A. § 895.481	X	X
Wyoming	WY Stat. § 1-1-122		

Important: Make sure to carefully read each equine liability law that applies where you do business and where you reside.